Agile Essentials

From Concepts to Customer Delight

RAHUL SHAH

Success is sweeter when shared with those who stood by you through every challenge.

To my wife, for your unwavering love, patience, and support that inspires me every day,

and to my parents, for your endless encouragement, wisdom, and belief in my dreams.

Hiral Shah

Narendrabhai Shah

Pritiben Shah

About the author

Rahul Shah is an **Agile Coach and Trainer** with over **24 years of experience** in Agile, Scrum, and Project Management. He specializes in making Agile principles **practical and accessible**, enabling teams and leaders to achieve **transformative results**.

Inspired by his love for **Chess, Sanskrit literature, Emotional Intelligence**, and the **Bhagavad Gita**, Rahul blends **strategy, wisdom**, and modern **Agile practices** into his coaching approach.

In this book *Agile Essentials: From Concepts to Customer Delight*, Rahul provides a **practical guide** to applying Agile in **real-world scenarios**. Using **metaphors** to simplify complex concepts, this book offers **actionable insights** for both beginners and experienced practitioners.

Rahul holds certifications including **SAFe SPC, PMP**, and **ICAgile Authorized Instructor for Agile Coaching**.

Preface

In today's fast-paced and ever-changing world, the ability to adapt and deliver results quickly has become a cornerstone of success. Agile project management has emerged as a powerful approach to achieve this, empowering teams to embrace change, prioritize value, and foster collaboration.

This book is born out of my passion for helping individuals and organizations understand and adopt Agile principles effectively. Over my years of experience in software development, I have seen both the triumphs and the pitfalls of Agile implementation. I realized that while many resources exist, there is often a gap in connecting Agile concepts with practical, real-world applications.

Agile Essentials aims to bridge that gap. It is designed for beginners stepping into the world of Agile and seasoned professionals seeking to refine their skills. The chapters take you through the essential principles, Scrum Framework, practical tools, and tips to overcome common challenges.

Whether you are a team member, project manager, or leader, my goal is to make this book your trusted guide in navigating Agile. By the time you finish, you will not only understand Agile but will also have the confidence to implement it successfully in your projects.

Thank you for embarking on this journey with me. I hope this book inspires you to unlock the true potential of Agile in your work and beyond.

With gratitude,

Rahul Shah

Agile Essentials: From Concepts to Customer Delight

Table of Contents

Chapter 1
Understanding Agile Fundamentals

1.1 What is Agile?

Imagine you are tasked with building a bridge. You plan every detail upfront, from materials to timelines, ensuring everything aligns perfectly. Now picture the weather changes, customer demands shift, or the river's flow alters unexpectedly. What happens to your rigid plan? It becomes obsolete.

This rigid plan reflects traditional project management models like **Waterfall**, where everything is predetermined. Now, imagine you build the bridge **incrementally** instead — adjusting to weather, customer feedback, and river changes along the way. You're flexible, adaptive, and responsive. This is **Agile**—a mindset and approach designed to embrace uncertainty, learn continuously, and focus on delivering value.

Agile is more than a methodology; it's a **philosophy** and way of working that allows teams to thrive in today's fast-changing, unpredictable world. At its heart, Agile emphasizes:
- **Flexibility** over rigid processes
- **Collaboration** over silos
- **Delivering value** in small increments

- **Continuous improvement** over fixed outcomes

Originally developed for software development, Agile's principles are now widely applied across industries like manufacturing, education, marketing, and personal productivity. Agile is about moving quickly while learning and improving continuously.

1.2 Why Agile?

We live in a **VUCA world**: volatile, uncertain, complex, and ambiguous. Organizations must deal with rapid technological changes, market fluctuations, and evolving customer expectations. Traditional approaches, like Waterfall, worked well when requirements were predictable and static, but they struggle in today's dynamic environment. A project cannot be considered successful if it meets the constraints of time, cost, and scope but fails to satisfy customer needs and expectations.

Agile is the Need of the Hour

In today's fast-paced environment, Agile is essential because it addresses key challenges faced by teams and organizations:

1. **Difficult to Get All Requirements Upfront**: Customers and stakeholders often cannot articulate their needs entirely at the beginning of a project.
2. **Requirements Are Bound to Change**: Market dynamics, technology, and customer expectations evolve, making initial plans obsolete.

3. **Limited Resources**: Organizations rarely have the time or budget to deliver everything, requiring a focus on prioritization.

Agile emerged as a solution to the chaos caused by rapidly changing requirements, limited resources, and unclear priorities. By focusing on iterative and incremental delivery, Agile ensures that teams concentrate on what truly matters—prioritizing tasks, adapting to change effectively, and consistently **delivering value**.

Key Benefits of Agile

1. **Faster Adaptation to Change:** Change is welcomed—even late in the process.
2. **Customer-Centric Approach:** Regular feedback ensures teams build what users actually need.
3. **Risk Management:** Working in short cycles identifies issues early, reducing costly rework.
4. **Incremental Value Delivery:** Teams deliver usable products frequently rather than waiting for a finished outcome.
5. **Improved Collaboration:** Agile promotes transparency, open communication, and teamwork.

Metaphor: Agile is like driving a car with a GPS—you adjust based on real-time feedback like traffic and weather. Waterfall, on the other hand, is like traveling by train—you follow a fixed path and cannot adapt to obstacles.

1.3 The 'Agile is Dead' Debate: A Critical Look

The Agile movement, once a revolutionary approach to

software development, has recently faced increasing scepticism. Critics claim that Agile is "dead," arguing that its principles have been diluted, misapplied, or overtaken by newer methodologies. This sub-chapter delves into the roots of the "Agile is Dead" narrative and examines the counterarguments defending Agile's continued relevance.

The Roots of the "Agile is Dead" Narrative

1. **Mis-implementation Across Organizations:** Many companies claim to be "Agile," yet they rigidly adhere to frameworks, resulting in bureaucratic processes that stifle the flexibility Agile was meant to foster. The essence of Agile is lost when organizations focus more on frameworks than on the principles driving them.

2. **Overabundance of Frameworks:** The proliferation of Agile frameworks—Scrum, Kanban, SAFe, LeSS, and many others—can be overwhelming. This complexity confuses organizations, reducing Agile to just a collection of tools instead of a mindset focused on collaboration, customer value, and continuous improvement.

3. **Dilution of Meaning:** As "Agile" becomes synonymous with any flexible approach, its original intent gets overshadowed, leading to scepticism about its effectiveness and whether it offers distinct advantages over traditional methods.

4. **Over-reliance on Certification as a Measure of Expertise:** The growing emphasis on certifications, particularly from short-term programs, often shifts

focus to credentials over actual knowledge and practical application, creating a false sense of expertise that hinders effective Agile adoption.

5. **Silver Bullet Mentality and "Doing" Agile vs. "Being" Agile:** Many organizations approach Agile adoption as a quick fix or silver bullet to solve all their problems. This mindset leads them to focus only on "doing" Agile—implementing frameworks and processes—without embracing the deeper, transformative shift of "being" Agile. The result is that they miss out on the true potential of Agile, which lies not just in following practices, but in adopting an Agile mindset.

Defending Agile's Vitality

Despite the criticisms, Agile's core principles continue to be highly relevant in today's fast-paced, ever-evolving business world.

1. **Core Principles Enduring:** Agile's core principles, such as flexibility, customer collaboration, and responsiveness to change, remain essential. They enable organizations to adapt quickly to changing market conditions, ensuring ongoing relevance and competitiveness in an uncertain world.

2. **Customer-Centric Focus:** Agile's commitment to delivering customer value through continuous feedback remains its strongest pillar. By listening to customers and iterating based on their needs, Agile organizations are able to build stronger, more

resilient relationships and maintain a competitive edge in the VUCA world.

3. **Integration with Modern Practices:** Agile is not static; it continuously evolves and integrates with modern practices like DevOps, Lean, and Continuous Delivery. This adaptability ensures Agile remains relevant not only in software development but also in other domains that require flexibility and responsiveness.

Facing Future Challenges

While Agile offers significant advantages, organizations must address several challenges to maintain its success.

1. **Cultural Shifts:** Adopting Agile demands a cultural shift within an organization, which can be a tough challenge. Shifting mindsets and deeply ingrained habits requires patience, leadership, and a willingness to embrace change.

2. **Long-Term Commitment:** Agile is not a one-time initiative but a long-term journey. Organizations need a sustained commitment to training, coaching, and ongoing improvement to truly reap the benefits of Agile methodologies.

3. **Effective Measurement:** To fully understand Agile's impact, organizations must develop robust metrics that go beyond surface-level. Focusing on the value delivered and how Agile contributes to organizational success can help validate its continued relevance and adoption.

Conclusion

The "Agile is Dead" debate serves as a critical reflection point for the Agile community. It underscores the challenges and misinterpretations Agile faces while reaffirming the enduring value of its core principles. By embracing Agile's continuous evolution and staying true to its foundational principles, organizations can ensure its longevity and effectiveness in the years to come.

1.4 History of Agile & the Agile Manifesto

The seeds of Agile were sown in the 1990s when software development faced a **crisis**:
- Projects were **slow to deliver** and often failed to meet customer expectations.
- Teams were burdened by overwhelming documentation instead of focusing on outcomes.
- Developers and business stakeholders worked in **silos**, leading to misalignment.

In February 2001, **17 software thought leaders** met in Snowbird, Utah, to address these issues. This gathering birthed the **Manifesto for Agile Software Development**, which revolutionized software development and project management.

Agile Manifesto

We are uncovering better ways of developing software by doing it and helping others do it. Through this work we have come to value:

Individuals and interactions over processes and tools

Working software over comprehensive documentation

Customer collaboration over contract negotiation

Responding to change over following a plan

While there is value in the items on the right, we value the items on the left more.

Source: https://www.academia.edu/

The Four Values of the Agile Manifesto

1. **Individuals and interactions** over processes and tools
2. **Working software** over comprehensive documentation
3. **Customer collaboration** over contract negotiation
4. **Responding to change** over following a plan

While Agile does not dismiss processes or documentation, it prioritizes people, collaboration, and outcomes because they are key to success.

The 12 Principles of Agile

1. **Our highest priority** is to satisfy the **customer** through early and continuous delivery of **valuable software.**
2. **Welcome changing requirements**, even late in development. Agile processes harness change for the customer's **competitive advantage**.
3. Deliver working software **frequently**, from a couple

of weeks to a couple of months, with a preference for the **shorter timescale**.

4. Business people and **developers** must work together **daily** throughout the project.
5. Build projects around **motivated individuals**. Give them the environment and support they need, and trust them to get the job done.
6. The most efficient and effective method of conveying information to and within a development team is **face-to-face conversation**.
7. **Working software** is the **primary measure** of progress.
8. Agile processes promote **sustainable development**. The sponsors, developers, and users should be able to maintain a **constant pace** indefinitely.
9. Continuous attention to **technical excellence** and good design enhances **agility**.
10. **Simplicity** – the art of maximizing the amount of work **not done** – is essential.
11. The best architectures, requirements, and designs emerge from **self-organizing teams**.
12. At regular intervals, the team reflects on how to become **more effective**, then tunes and adjusts its Behaviour **accordingly**.

These values and principles are the **North Star** for Agile teams, guiding their Behaviour and decision-making.

1.5 Key Agile Frameworks

Agile is an **umbrella term** that encompasses a broad set of values, principles, and frameworks designed to enable teams to work iteratively, collaboratively, and adaptively. The **Manifesto for Agile Software Development** and its values and principles provide the foundation for all Agile practices. Over time, several frameworks have been developed under the Agile umbrella to help teams put these principles into practice effectively. The most popular frameworks include:

1. Scrum

- **What It Is**: A lightweight, iterative framework that focuses on delivering **incremental value** through short time-boxed iterations called **Sprints** (typically 1–4 weeks).
- **Key Components**:
  - **Roles**: Product Owner, Scrum Master, Development Team
  - **Events**: Sprint Planning, Daily Standup, Sprint Review, Sprint Retrospective
  - **Artifacts**: Product Backlog, Sprint Backlog, Increment
- **When to Use**: Best for projects with rapidly changing requirements and a need for regular feedback.

2. Kanban

- **What It Is**: A **visual framework** that focuses on managing workflow and improving efficiency by limiting **Work-in-Progress (WIP)**.

- **Key Components:**
    - o **Kanban Board**: Visual tool with columns (To-Do, In Progress, Done)
    - o **WIP Limits**: Limits on how many tasks can be in a particular column
    - o **Continuous Flow**: Tasks move through the board at their own pace
- **When to Use**: Best for teams needing continuous delivery or dealing with unpredictable work (e.g., support or maintenance teams)

3. Extreme Programming (XP)

- **What It Is**: A software development framework emphasizing **engineering practices** to improve software quality and responsiveness to changing requirements.
- **Key Practices:**
    - o **Pair Programming**: Two developers work together on the same code
    - o **Test-Driven Development (TDD)**: Writing tests before writing code
    - o **Continuous Integration**: Frequently merging code changes into a shared repository
    - o **Refactoring**: Improving code without changing its Behaviour
- **When to Use**: Ideal for projects requiring high-quality software with rapidly changing requirements.

4. Lean Software Development

- **What It Is**: Based on **Lean manufacturing principles**, Lean focuses on eliminating **waste**, optimizing flow, and delivering value faster.
- **Key Principles**:
    - Eliminate Waste
    - Build Quality In
    - Amplify Learning
    - Deliver Fast
    - Empower the Team
    - Decide Late (last responsible moment)
    - Optimize the Whole
- **When to Use**: Best for teams looking to streamline their processes and minimize inefficiencies

5. Disciplined Agile Delivery (DAD)

- **What It Is**: A process decision framework that provides teams with a **goal-based approach** for choosing the best Agile practices.
- **Key Elements**:
    - Combines practices from Scrum, Kanban, Lean, and DevOps
    - Focuses on the full delivery lifecycle
    - Flexible approach tailored to organizational needs
- **When to Use**: Best for teams looking for flexibility and guidance to mix-and-match Agile techniques

6. Feature-Driven Development (FDD)

- **What It Is**: An Agile framework focused on delivering **features** (small, client-valued functionalities) incrementally.
- **Key Practices**:
    - Develop an Overall Model
    - Build a Features List
    - Plan by Feature
    - Design by Feature
    - Build by Feature
- **When to Use**: Best for larger teams working on feature-heavy projects.

7. Crystal

- **What It Is**: A family of Agile frameworks (e.g., Crystal Clear, Crystal Yellow, Crystal Orange) tailored to teams of different sizes and criticality.
- **Core Focus**: People, communication, and interaction over rigid processes.
- **When to Use**: Best for smaller teams prioritizing team communication and project simplicity.

While Agile itself is a **philosophy**, these frameworks provide concrete practices and structures for implementing Agile principles in real-world projects.

In this book, we will focus heavily on **Scrum**, the most widely adopted Agile framework that balances simplicity with effectiveness, making it ideal for teams seeking high-value delivery and continuous improvement.

1.6 Agile vs. Waterfall: A Comparative Analysis

The **Waterfall model** was the traditional approach to project management, where the project flows linearly through distinct phases such as **requirements gathering, design, development, testing, and deployment**.

Once a phase is completed, it's difficult to go back and make changes. In contrast, **Agile** embraces flexibility and iterative progress. Let's break down the key differences between Agile and Waterfall:

Aspect	Agile	Waterfall
Approach	Iterative and incremental	Linear and sequential
Flexibility	Highly adaptable to change	Rigid and resistant to change
Customer Involvement	Continuous collaboration and feedback	Limited to start and end phases
Delivery	Frequent, small increments	Delivered all at once at the end
Documentation	Minimal, focused on working outcomes	Comprehensive and mandatory

	Faster, value delivered incrementally	Slower, value delivered at completion
Time to Market		

To truly appreciate the benefits of Agile, let us compare it with traditional approaches like **Waterfall**. The following visual comparison illustrates how Agile and Waterfall differ across four critical dimensions: **Visibility**, **Ability to Change**, **Business Value**, and **Risk** over time.

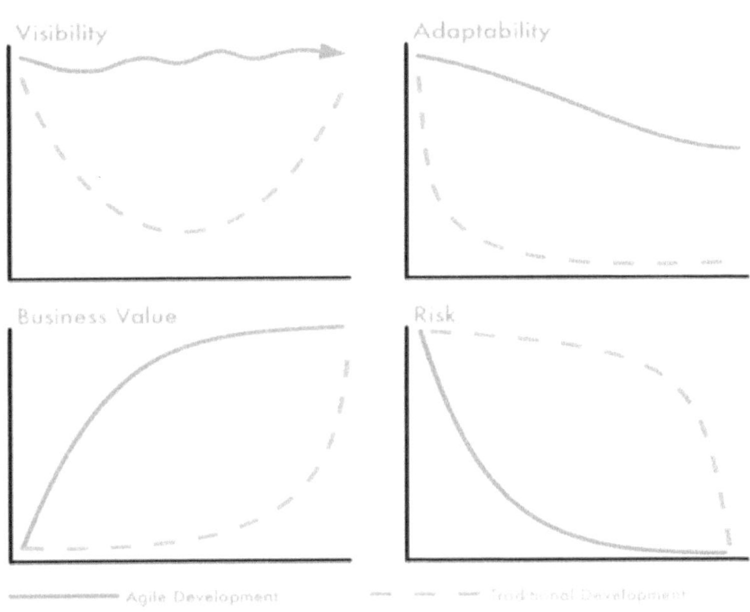

Source: https://medium.com/agileinsider/

This comparison highlights how Agile and Waterfall differ across **Visibility**, **Ability to Change**, **Business Value**, and **Risk** over time:

1. **Visibility**: In Waterfall, visibility starts high during planning but drops until the end, creating uncertainty. Agile ensures consistent visibility through regular feedback loops and iterative deliveries.
2. **Ability to Change**: Waterfall becomes rigid over time, making changes costly and disruptive. Agile embraces change, maintaining flexibility throughout the project to meet evolving needs.
3. **Business Value**: Waterfall delivers value only at the end, delaying benefits. Agile provides incremental value early and continuously, ensuring features align with business priorities.
4. **Risk**: Risks in Waterfall persist until late phases when testing occurs. Agile minimizes risk through frequent testing, feedback, and adjustments, reducing issues progressively over time.

Key Insight: Agile's iterative approach provides continuous value, transparency, and adaptability, making it a powerful alternative to Waterfall's linear and rigid structure.

Metaphor:

Waterfall is like building a house where every detail is planned upfront. If the blueprint needs changes, it's costly and time-consuming. Agile, however, is like renovating a house room by room—you adapt plans based on real-time feedback while still delivering value incrementally.

Agile is not just a methodology—it's a mindset shift designed to address the needs of today's dynamic and fast-paced world. By understanding its origins, values, and comparative benefits, you now have a solid foundation to explore Agile in practice.

In the next chapter, we'll dive into the **Agile mindset and philosophy** to understand how adopting a growth-oriented approach enables teams and individuals to succeed.

Reflective Questions

1. What is one situation in your work or life where adaptability and flexibility led to a better outcome? How does this align with the Agile mindset?
2. Which of the four Agile values do you find most challenging to apply? Why?
3. How would adopting an Agile approach improve a recent or ongoing project compared to using a traditional Waterfall approach?
4. Think about the 12 Agile Principles—what is one principle you can start applying immediately to improve your team's performance?
5. If you had to choose between Scrum and Kanban for managing unpredictable work, which framework would you choose and why?
6. How does the comparison between driving with a GPS (Agile) and following a fixed train track (Waterfall) apply to the way you or your organization currently operate?

Chapter 2
The Agile Mindset and Philosophy

2.1 Fixed vs. Growth Mindset

In Agile, the focus is not just on processes, tools, or frameworks, but also on the **mindset** that teams and individuals bring to their work. The **Agile mindset** is rooted in a **growth mindset**, a term popularized by psychologist **Carol Dweck**.

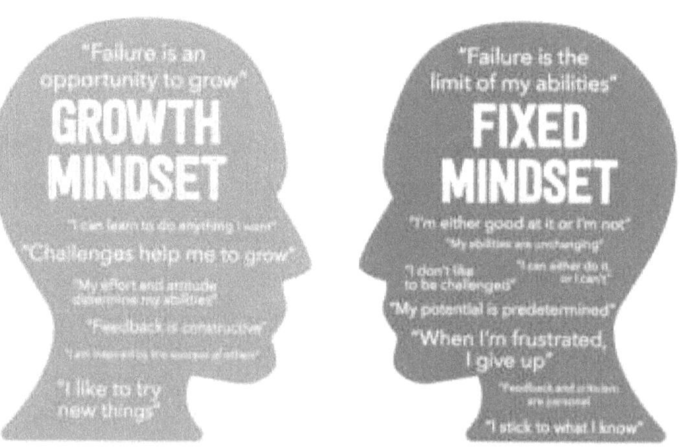

Sources: https://medium.com/leadership-motivation-and-impact/fixed-v-growth-mindset-902e7d0081b3

Fixed Mindset vs. Growth Mindset

- **Fixed Mindset:** Individuals with a fixed mindset believe that their abilities are **static,** and that success is determined by innate talent. They avoid challenges, give up easily, and see effort as fruitless. They fear failure and often give up quickly.

- **Growth Mindset:** In contrast, those with a growth mindset believe that abilities can be **developed** through dedication, learning, and hard work. They embrace challenges, persist through obstacles, and see failure as an opportunity for growth.

In Agile, a growth mindset is essential because it promotes **continuous learning** and **improvement**. Agile teams are encouraged to experiment, fail fast, and adapt. The goal is to keep learning and improving iteratively. This mindset shift is what allows individuals and teams to thrive in dynamic, unpredictable environments.

How Agile Encourages a Growth Mindset

Agile provides an environment where failure is seen not as a setback but as an opportunity to learn and adapt. The regular **retrospectives** (in Scrum, for example) offer a structured approach to reviewing both successes and failures. Teams are encouraged to ask:

- What worked well?
- What can we improve next time?
- How can we adjust our approach to enhance outcomes?

This constant reflection and adaptation create a culture of growth, where challenges are seen as opportunities to innovate, develop new solutions, and refine practices.

2.2 Adopting an Agile Mindset

Adopting an Agile mindset is not just about **following practices**—it's about embracing a fundamental change in how you approach work. It's a shift from **predicting** outcomes to **responding** to emerging needs. Here's how you can start adopting this mindset:

1. **Embrace Change:** Instead of fearing change, see it as an opportunity for improvement. Agile encourages responsiveness to changes in customer needs, technology, and market dynamics.
2. **Collaborate Continuously:** Agile emphasizes team collaboration over individual effort. Be open to sharing ideas, learning from others, and working together toward a common goal.
3. **Focus on Value Delivery:** Agile puts the emphasis on **delivering value** to the customer, not just completing tasks. Each iteration should deliver something that brings real value to the customer or end-user.
4. **Prioritize Transparency:** In Agile, transparency is key. Everyone in the team should have a clear understanding of the project's vision, progress, challenges, and goals. This enables effective collaboration and decision-making.

Developing an Agile Mindset as a Team

While the Agile mindset starts with individuals, it is nurtured and maintained at the **team level**. A team that adopts an

Agile mindset will:

- **Solve problems collectively**, using the diverse perspectives and expertise within the group.
- **Experiment** and iterate, making continuous improvements to processes and deliverables.
- **Focus on results**, not just output, ensuring that every action leads toward delivering value to customers.

It's crucial to create a **safe environment** where team members can speak up, challenge assumptions, and provide constructive feedback. This openness fosters creativity and encourages teams to experiment, fail, and learn.

In a nutshell, Agile is a mindset defined by four values, supported by twelve principles, and manifested through numerous practices and frameworks.

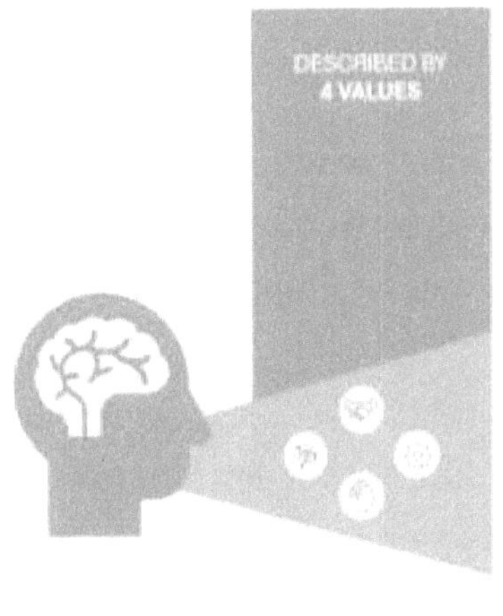

Metaphor:
The Agile mindset is like navigating a river. Just as a river constantly flows and adapts to the environment around it, an Agile approach requires constant learning and adaptation. You may face obstacles, such as rocks or fast-moving waters, but your ability to steer around them, learn from each twist and turn, and adjust your course reflects the growth mindset necessary for success in Agile.

2.3 The Role of Emotional Intelligence in Agile

An often-overlooked aspect of the Agile mindset is the role of **Emotional Intelligence (EI)** in driving success. Emotional intelligence is the ability to recognize, understand, and manage our emotions and the emotions of others. In Agile environments, where collaboration, adaptability, and strong relationships are essential, Emotional Intelligence (EI) becomes a key factor for success.

Key components of Emotional Intelligence
1. **Self-awareness** helps Agile team members identify their strengths and weaknesses, improving their ability to contribute effectively.
2. **Self-regulation** ensures that individuals remain calm and focused, especially during difficult situations or when things don't go as planned.
3. **Motivation** drives individuals to persist through challenges and setbacks, a key trait for Agile teams that work in fast-changing environments.

4. **Empathy** fosters understanding and collaboration between team members and customers, leading to better communication and stronger relationships.
5. **Social skills** enable teams to work together harmoniously, resolving conflicts and improving team dynamics.

How to Develop Emotional Intelligence in Agile

The *CARE* model provides a simple, actionable framework for developing EI and fostering positive team dynamics. It stands for:

- **C: Connect with Empathy**
  This step encourages **active listening**—paying full attention to what others are saying, without interrupting. It's about understanding their feelings and perspective before offering solutions. Show empathy by acknowledging emotions and responding in ways that convey understanding.
- **A: Acknowledge Emotions**
  Recognizing and validating emotions helps to create an open, supportive atmosphere. Reflect on your own emotions and how they might influence your responses. By practicing **mindfulness**, you can remain calm and thoughtful, even during stressful moments. Saying things like, "It's okay to feel this way," fosters trust and openness.
- **R: Respond Constructively**
  In this step, focus on **encouraging open**

communication and offering solutions, rather than reacting impulsively. Use **I** statements, such as "I feel... because..." to express concerns without blame. Instead of retreating into withdrawal, ensure that communication remains open and that you respond with clear, actionable next steps. Conflict is inevitable, but with EI, it becomes an opportunity for growth. Use your conflict resolution skills to ensure all voices are heard and navigate difficult conversations.

- **E: Elevate Relationships**
  This step is about strengthening relationships through **appreciation** and trust-building. Praise team members with specific, timely feedback like, "Your analysis was insightful." Follow through on commitments to demonstrate reliability. By elevating relationships, you not only build trust but also cultivate an environment where transparency, a core Agile value, thrives.

By incorporating the *CARE* model, Agile teams can enhance Emotional Intelligence, improve communication, and foster stronger collaboration—ultimately leading to greater success in delivering customer value

2.4 The Agile Mindset Beyond Work

The Agile mindset doesn't just apply to the workplace—it can also be integrated into your **personal life**. In fact, many of the principles of Agile can be beneficial in navigating the complexities of personal development, relationships, and decision-making.

Applying Agile to Personal Life

1. **Iterative Growth:** Just as Agile encourages continuous improvement in projects, you can apply the same principle to your personal goals. Instead of striving for perfection from the start, focus on incremental progress. For example, if you're learning a new skill, aim for small wins each day.

2. **Feedback Loops:** Regularly reflect on your progress and adjust based on feedback—whether from yourself or others. This helps you stay aligned with your goals and adjust when things aren't working.

3. **Value-Driven Decisions:** In Agile, every decision is made with the customer's value in mind. Similarly, in your personal life, ask yourself: "Will this decision bring me closer to my goals or values?"

4. **Collaboration in Personal Relationships:** Agile values collaboration, so why not apply this in your personal relationships? Share your goals with others, collaborate on solutions, and provide support when needed.

Living the Agile Mindset Daily

The Agile mindset is about **embracing change, learning continuously**, and **delivering value**. By adopting these principles in both your professional and personal life, you can navigate challenges with more resilience, clarity, and purpose. Living with an Agile mindset leads to greater Fulfilment and success—both at work and in life.

Reflective Questions

1. Which elements of a **growth mindset** can you apply to your work and personal life?
2. How can you encourage your team to adopt a growth mindset?
3. In what ways can **emotional intelligence** improve your team's collaboration and outcomes?
4. How can you integrate **Agile principles** into your daily life to achieve better results and personal growth?
5. How can you use the *CARE* model to enhance your approach in the next team interaction?

Chapter 3
Understanding the Scrum Framework

This chapter delves into the core elements of Scrum, including its three foundational pillars and the Scrum values that guide teams to successful outcomes.

3.1 What is Scrum?

Scrum is a lightweight framework that helps people, teams, and organizations generate value through adaptive solutions for complex problems. Developed by Jeff Sutherland and Ken Schwaber in the 1990s, Scrum offers a structured yet flexible approach that fosters collaboration, accountability, and iterative progress toward clear goals.

Widely adopted across various industries for its simplicity, effectiveness, and focus on continuous improvement, Scrum organizes work into short, time-boxed iterations called Sprints.

"Scrum is like a rugby game, not a relay race."
In Scrum, the emphasis is on continuous teamwork and adaptability. Like a rugby match, the entire team works together to move the ball forward, adjusting tactics as needed. Unlike a relay race, where one runner hands off the baton, Scrum teams collaborate throughout the process, ensuring that everyone remains engaged and adjusts their

approach based on feedback and evolving requirements. This collective effort is at the heart of Scrum's iterative approach, empowering cross-functional teams to deliver value incrementally.

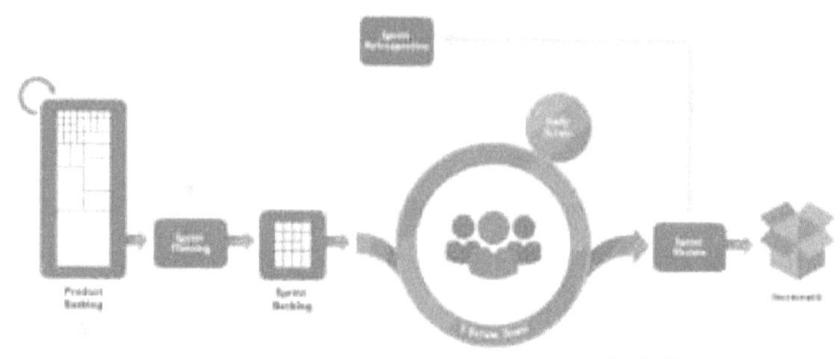

Source: https://www.scrum.org/resources/scrum-framework-poster

Scrum operates under the broader Agile umbrella. While Agile defines a set of values and principles for managing projects, Scrum provides specific roles, events, and artifacts that operationalize these principles. Other Agile methodologies, like Kanban, Extreme Programming (XP), and Lean, offer alternative approaches, but Scrum remains one of the most popular frameworks due to its structured nature.

Key Characteristics of Scrum:
- **Iterative and Incremental:**
  Scrum divides work into short Sprints, delivering small, valuable increments regularly. This approach

ensures continuous improvement and frequent delivery, allowing teams to respond quickly to changes.

- **Empirical Process Control:**
Scrum relies on **transparency**, **inspection**, and **adaptation**. Decisions are based on real data and observations, with teams regularly reviewing progress and adjusting to improve the product and process.

- **People-Centric:**
Scrum empowers teams to take ownership of their work. It fosters collaboration, accountability, and creativity, encouraging individuals to contribute to team success and building a culture of trust and respect.

Benefits of Understanding Scrum Fundamentals

Mastering Scrum fundamentals equips teams with the tools and mindset to thrive in dynamic environments. Some benefits include:

- **Improved Collaboration**: Clear roles and structured events promote teamwork.
- **Faster Delivery**: Iterative delivery leads to faster time-to-market.
- **Enhanced Quality**: Regular inspections allow teams to identify and fix issues early.
- **Customer Satisfaction**: Incremental delivery and continuous feedback ensure alignment with

customer needs.

3.2 The Three Pillars of Scrum

Scrum is built upon three pillars—Transparency, Inspection, and Adaptation—that ensure teams remain aligned, informed, and responsive to change.

1. Transparency

Transparency means making all aspects of the Scrum process visible to those responsible for the outcome. When everyone has a clear understanding of the work, decisions are based on shared knowledge, allowing teams to address issues before they escalate.

- **Artifacts and Events**: Scrum artifacts (such as the Product Backlog, Sprint Backlog, and Increment) and events promote transparency by keeping everyone informed about the status of work.
- **Metaphor**: Imagine a glasshouse where every plant's growth is visible to all. In Scrum, transparency serves as the "glass," enabling teams and stakeholders to observe progress and identify issues early.

2. Inspection

Inspection is the act of regularly reviewing Scrum artifacts and the team's progress toward the Sprint Goal. Frequent inspection helps identify deviations, obstacles, or risks that need attention.

- **Key Events for Inspection**:

- o **Daily Scrum**: A quick, daily check-in where team members assess their progress and make adjustments.
- o **Sprint Review**: A meeting at the end of each Sprint to review the Increment and gather feedback from stakeholders. Similarly, the other events also provide an opportunity for inspection.
- **Metaphor**: Think of a pilot regularly checking flight instruments. Similarly, Scrum teams inspect their progress to stay on course and ensure alignment with the goal.

3. Adaptation

Adaptation is the response to inspection. When teams identify deviations or areas for improvement, they adjust their work processes or goals to improve outcomes.

- **Responding to Change**: Scrum emphasizes flexibility and encourages teams to pivot quickly when necessary, ensuring alignment with customer needs and project objectives.
- **Metaphor**: Imagine a sailor adjusting their sails based on changing wind directions. Just like this, Scrum teams adapt their strategies and approach to navigate challenges effectively.

All events and artifacts in Scrum provide opportunities for **inspection** and **adaptation**, while acting as vehicles for **transparency**. This iterative process drives Scrum teams toward higher performance, greater collaboration, and the delivery of better value to the customer.

3.3 Scrum Values

Scrum is underpinned by five core values that guide decision-making, Behaviour, and collaboration within Scrum teams. These values foster a culture of respect, accountability, and continuous improvement.

1. **Commitment**: Scrum teams are dedicated to achieving their goals and supporting each other in delivering value.
2. **Focus**: Teams concentrate on high-priority tasks, ensuring minimal distractions and optimal value delivery.
3. **Openness**: Transparent communication fosters trust and collaboration among team members and stakeholders.
4. **Respect**: Team members value each other's perspectives and contributions, creating an environment of mutual trust.
5. **Courage**: Teams are empowered to make difficult decisions, voice concerns, and try new approaches.

Metaphor for Scrum Values: Think of a strong bridge held up by five pillars. Each pillar—Commitment, Focus, Openness, Respect, and Courage—supports the team, allowing them to cross the journey of ideation to delivery successfully.

3.4 Scrum Roles and Responsibilities

Scrum defines three key roles, each with specific responsibilities that ensure the framework's success. These roles collaborate closely to deliver value efficiently.

1. Product Owner

The Product Owner is responsible for maximizing the value of the product by managing the Product Backlog. They prioritize work, articulate the vision, and represent the voice of the customer to ensure the team focuses on the most valuable tasks.

- **Responsibilities**:
    - Prioritize the backlog based on business value and customer needs.
    - Articulate the vision and goals for the product.
    - Ensure backlog items are well-defined and understood by the team.
    - Ensure the Scrum team works on the most valuable tasks first.
    - Regularly communicate with stakeholders to gather feedback.
- **Metaphor**: The Product Owner acts as a compass, guiding the team toward customer satisfaction while navigating changing landscapes and requirements.

2. Scrum Master

The Scrum Master is a servant-leader who facilitates the Scrum process, removes impediments, and ensures the team follows Scrum principles. They help the team improve continuously and protect it from external disruptions.

- **Responsibilities**:
    - Facilitate Scrum events.
    - Coach the team on Agile practices and principles.
    - Assist the Product Owner in managing and prioritizing the backlog
    - Help the team to become more effective in their delivery and collaboration
    - Protect the team from external disruptions and distractions.
    - Assist in organizational changes and support the implementation of scrum
- **Metaphor**: The Scrum Master is like a gardener, creating an environment where the team (plants) can thrive by removing obstacles (weeds) and providing support (nourishment).

3. Developers

Developers are cross-functional team members who work collaboratively to deliver a potentially shippable Increment at the end of each Sprint. They take ownership of the work and self-organize to achieve the Sprint Goal.

- **Responsibilities**:
    - Plan and execute tasks to meet Sprint

commitments.
- o   Ensure a potentially shippable product increment is delivered by the end of each Sprint.
- o   Collaborate closely with the Product Owner and Scrum Master.
- o   Decide how best to organize their work to ensure flexibility and efficiency
- o   Ensure the quality and completeness of the Increment.
- **Metaphor**: Developers are the builders of a house, laying bricks and constructing walls while ensuring the structure aligns with the blueprint.

3.5 Scrum Events (ceremonies)

Scrum events are the structured meetings that facilitate communication, transparency, and progress within the team. These events are essential for keeping the team focused and aligned toward achieving the sprint goal.

1. The Sprint: A Sprint is the heartbeat of Scrum during which all other events occur. It is a fixed-length iteration, typically lasting 1 to 4 weeks, during which a specific set of work is completed. Each Sprint includes several key activities.
- **Purpose**: Deliver value incrementally and iteratively.
- **Key Features**:
  - o   Time-boxed.

- o   At the end of each sprint, a potentially shippable product increment is delivered.
  - o   Each sprint has a goal to achieve.
- **Metaphor**: The Sprint is like running a race, where consistent effort and focus help the team.

2. Sprint Planning

Sprint Planning occurs at the start of each sprint. During this meeting, the Scrum Team collaborates to define the Sprint Goal, select Product Backlog items for the Sprint Backlog, and determine how to deliver those items.

- **Inputs**: Product Backlog, team capacity, and historical performance.
- **Key Features**:
  - o   Define the Sprint Goal.
  - o   Prioritize and break down Product Backlog items.
  - o   Determine the tasks required to complete the work.
- **Outputs**: Sprint Goal, selected backlog items, and a plan for execution.
- **Metaphor**: Sprint Planning is like setting the itinerary for a road trip, ensuring everyone knows the destination and route.

3. Daily Scrum

The Daily Scrum is a short, time-boxed meeting (usually 15 minutes) that occurs every day during the sprint. The Development Team provides updates on their progress, plans for the day, and any obstacles they are facing. The Daily Scrum takes place at the same time and location every day.

- **Purpose**: Identify roadblocks, align efforts, and adapt plans as necessary.
- **Key Features**:
  - Focus on progress toward the Sprint Goal.
  - Each team member answers three questions: What did you do yesterday? What will you do today? Are there any obstacles? This is just a suggested format—teams are encouraged to be creative in conducting the Daily Scrum to accelerate progress toward the sprint goal.
  - Helps with coordination, inspection, aids in planning for the next day and identifies blockers early.
- **Metaphor**: The Daily Scrum is like a pit stop in a race, where the team checks the car (progress) and makes quick adjustments.

4. Sprint Review

At the end of the sprint, the Scrum Team holds a Sprint Review to inspect the Increment and adapt the Product Backlog if necessary. The team demonstrates the work completed during the sprint to stakeholders and gathers feedback.

- **Focus**: Inspect the Increment, adapt the Product Backlog, and celebrate achievements.
- **Key Features**:
  - Review the Increment and get feedback.
  - Reassess the Product Backlog based on the

review.

- o Collaborate with stakeholders to ensure alignment.
- **Metaphor**: The Sprint Review is like unveiling a new dish to diners, collecting their feedback to improve the recipe.

5. Sprint Retrospective

The Sprint Retrospective occurs after the Sprint Review and before the next Sprint Planning. It provides the team with an opportunity to reflect on the sprint, identify what went well, and find areas for improvement.

- **Goal**: Foster continuous improvement and boost team morale.
- **Key Features**:
  - o Inspect the team's processes, collaboration, and tools.
  - o Identify successes and areas for improvement.
  - o Create action plans for improvement in the next sprint.
- **Metaphor**: The Retrospective is like looking into a mirror, helping the team make adjustments for future success.

3.6 Scrum Artifacts

Scrum relies on several artifacts to provide transparency and track progress throughout the project. These artifacts represent key information for the team and stakeholders.

- **Product Backlog**:
    - The Product Backlog is an ordered list of all desired features, enhancements, fixes, and work required to deliver a product. It is managed by the Product Owner and is continuously updated as the project evolves.
    - **Key Features**:
        - Dynamic and evolving throughout the project.
        - Prioritized by business value and urgency.
        - Items are refined over time, known as "backlog refinement (grooming)."

- **Sprint Backlog**:
    - The Sprint Backlog is a subset of the Product Backlog, consisting of the items that the team commits to completing during a specific sprint. It is owned by the Development Team, who break down backlog items into tasks and estimate them.
    - **Key Features**:
        - Items are selected during Sprint Planning.
        - Focuses on tasks to achieve the sprint goal.
        - May evolve throughout the sprint as needed.

- **Increment**:
  - Scrum believes in delivering incremental value for faster feedback. The Increment is the sum of all the work completed during the current sprint, combined with the work completed in previous sprints. It must be in a usable state, regardless of whether the Product Owner decides to release it.

  - **Key Features**:
    - Represents a potentially shippable product.
    - Demonstrates progress and provides stakeholders with a tangible outcome.

In this chapter, we explored the foundational aspects of the Scrum framework, including its key pillars of Transparency, Inspection, and Adaptation, as well as the core values that guide teams toward success. We examined how Scrum empowers teams through its iterative and collaborative approach, fostering continuous improvement and value delivery. Additionally, we delved into the roles, events, and artifacts that structure Scrum, providing a clear framework for managing complex projects and ensuring customer satisfaction.

Reflective Questions:

1. How do the roles of Product Owner, Scrum Master,

and Developers complement each other in Scrum?

2. Why is the Daily Scrum critical for maintaining team alignment?

3. Which Scrum event do you find most valuable, and why?

4. How do Scrum values impact team collaboration and decision-making?

5. How might adopting Scrum benefit your organization's ability to navigate change?

Chapter 4
Iterative Development and Continuous Improvement

In the world of Agile, development isn't a single, linear sprint towards a fixed goal; it's a dynamic journey that evolves over time. Picture it like navigating a winding road with frequent pit stops to assess your direction, adjust the route, and refine your vehicle. Each step forward is a chance to improve, learn, and deliver greater value. At the heart of this journey are **iterative development** and **continuous improvement**—two essential practices that empower teams to stay flexible, adapt to change, and increase performance.

4.1 The Power of Small, Incremental Steps

In Agile, large, complex challenges are tackled through small, manageable chunks. Instead of spending months building a massive deliverable, Scrum breaks work into short, focused periods known as Sprints. These time-boxed iterations—usually lasting two to four weeks—allow teams to make steady, continuous progress toward their goal.

Unlike traditional project management, where progress can often feel like a long haul with little feedback until the end, Agile's iterative development offers regular opportunities to pause, reflect, and adjust. This approach keeps teams on track and responsive to customer needs.

Think of it like building a puzzle: instead of waiting until every piece is in place to see the final picture, you work on one small section at a time, evaluating and adjusting as you go. Every small section brings you closer to the complete image, and if something doesn't quite fit, it's easy to make changes early in the process.

Benefits of Iterative Development:

- **Quicker Feedback:** Teams receive immediate feedback, ensuring they remain aligned with customer needs and expectations.
- **Risk Mitigation:** By delivering in small chunks, potential issues are identified sooner and addressed more quickly.
- **Increased Flexibility:** With each iteration, teams can adapt their approach based on new insights or shifting priorities.
- **Continuous Learning:** Each iteration is an opportunity to refine processes, implement lessons learned, and improve team performance.

4.2 Inspect and Adapt: The Agile Feedback Loop

At the core of Scrum is the principle of **Inspect and Adapt**, which drives continuous improvement and helps teams align with evolving goals, customer needs, and challenges. Unlike traditional models where progress is evaluated only at the end, Scrum embeds **inspection and adaptation** opportunities into all its events—ensuring teams learn, adjust, and improve frequently.

Every Scrum event acts as a checkpoint for transparency, inspection, and adaptation:

- **Sprint Planning**: The team inspects the Product Backlog to determine the most valuable work for the upcoming Sprint. By collaborating with the Product Owner, the team adapts the plan to align with priorities and the team's capacity. This event ensures clarity on *what* needs to be done and *how* to achieve it.
- **Daily Scrum**: This short, focused meeting is the heartbeat of inspection and adaptation. The team inspects their progress toward the Sprint Goal and adapts their daily plan to stay on track. It's like a navigator checking their route and making minor adjustments to avoid getting off course.
- **Sprint Review**: At the end of the Sprint, the team inspects the increment (what has been delivered) with stakeholders and adapts the Product Backlog based on feedback. This event helps ensure the product continues to meet stakeholder and business needs.
- **Sprint Retrospective**: This is the team's dedicated time to inspect *how* they worked together and identify improvements. It's about fine-tuning processes, communication, and collaboration to work better in the future.

Think of these events as regular *pit stops* in a long race. The team pauses briefly to check their progress, refuel, and make critical adjustments before moving forward with renewed focus and direction. Without these frequent pauses for inspection and adaptation, a team could drift off track and deliver less value.

The Power of Continuous Feedback

The feedback loop created by Scrum events ensures that teams operate in a cycle of learning and growth. Each event allows the team to observe their progress, gather insights, and adjust their plans, processes, or product as needed.

The **inspect and adapt** mindset enables teams to:

- **Identify problems early** and resolve them before they escalate.
- **Stay aligned** with business goals and customer expectations.
- **Increase agility** by responding to changes efficiently.
- **Continuously improve** their processes and team dynamics.

Ultimately, Scrum treats change as an opportunity, not a disruption. By embedding inspection and adaptation into every event, teams can deliver value consistently while learning and evolving every step of the way.

4.3 Creating a Culture of Continuous Improvement

In the world of Agile, continuous improvement is the lifeblood that keeps teams thriving and growing. It's not just about delivering a working product; it's about fostering a mindset where every step forward is an opportunity to grow, refine, and excel. Agile teams aim to deliver value regularly while improving how they work, ensuring that their processes, skills, and outcomes continuously evolve.

Imagine a gardener tending to a lush garden. Every day, they prune overgrown branches, nurture budding flowers, and enrich the soil. Just as the garden thrives through small, consistent efforts, Agile teams flourish by making incremental adjustments that compound into substantial growth over time.

Principles of Continuous Improvement:

1. **Reflect and Adjust**: Regular retrospectives serve as the gardener's pruning shears, allowing teams to trim inefficiencies and nurture best practices. By assessing what worked, what didn't, and what can be improved, teams adapt to challenges and enhance their workflows.

2. **Build Quality In**: Quality in Agile isn't an afterthought; it's like planting seeds with care from the very beginning. From writing clear, prioritized backlog items to ensuring high-quality code, teams embed quality into every stage of development.

3. **Empower the Team**:
   Just as a garden thrives with diverse plants working together, Agile teams flourish when each member takes ownership of the product's quality. Empowered individuals contribute to a collective sense of responsibility and pride in their work.

4. **Small, Incremental Changes**:
   Agile teams know that monumental transformations are often the result of small, consistent actions. Like the gardener's daily efforts, these small improvements compound over time, creating a resilient and high-performing team.

5. **Experimentation and Innovation**:
   Experimentation acts as the gardener's experimentation with new planting techniques. By testing innovative ideas and techniques, teams discover new ways to optimize their work and achieve better outcomes.

6. **Focus on Skill Development**:
   Investing in skill development is like enriching the soil with nutrients. By fostering growth through training, mentoring, and collaboration, teams cultivate adaptability and expertise, preparing for challenges in an ever-changing environment.

The Agile Symphony: Feedback and Collaboration

Continuous improvement thrives on feedback. Listening to

stakeholders, customers, and teammates is akin to observing how the garden responds to care. Feedback provides clarity on what's thriving and what needs attention, helping teams adapt to shifting requirements and expectations.

Continuous improvement is the melody that Agile teams dance to. It's a journey, not a destination—a commitment to constant learning, collaboration, and growth. With each Sprint, like the sculptor's careful chiselling or the gardener's nurturing touch, Agile teams move closer to delivering products and processes of unparalleled quality.

By embracing these core principles of Agile—iterative development, regular inspection, and continuous improvement—teams not only deliver better products but also foster a culture of collaboration, learning, and growth. It's a journey, not a destination, where each step forward enhances the end result.

Reflective Questions:
1. How do incremental steps contribute to continuous improvement in Agile?
2. How does regular inspection and adaptation improve the development process?
3. How does your team currently identify and act on opportunities for improvement in your processes and outcomes, and what can you do to make this approach more effective?

4. How do small adjustments in development practices enhance team performance?
5. What role does feedback play in the iterative process of Agile?
6. In what ways are you ensuring that the improvements you make deliver tangible value to your organization and clients?

Chapter 5
Building High-Performing Agile Teams

High-performing Agile teams are the backbone of successful product development. These teams drive innovation, deliver value, and adapt continuously. However, creating such teams requires attention to the dynamics, Behaviours, and communication patterns within the team.

In this chapter, we will explore what high-performing teams look like, drawing on Patrick Lencioni's *The Five Dysfunctions of a Team*. We will also discuss key characteristics, emotional intelligence (EI), conflict resolution, and the importance of fostering a culture of continuous improvement.

5.1 What Does a High-Performing Team Look Like?

A high-performing Agile team is a cohesive group that works seamlessly toward common goals. These teams display key characteristics:

Clear Purpose and Vision
High-performing teams share a clear understanding of their goals and the customer needs. Every member knows how their work contributes to the larger picture, creating focus and motivation. Alignment on purpose helps teams stay

committed, especially when challenges arise.

Trust and Psychological Safety

As per *The Five Dysfunctions of a Team*, trust is the foundation of high-performing teams. Trust enables team members to express ideas, admit mistakes, and ask for help without fear. Psychological safety, built through transparency, fosters collaboration and problem-solving, crucial for Agile success.

Open Communication and Transparency

Effective communication is central to high-performing teams. Transparency in progress, challenges, and ideas ensures everyone is aligned. Regular Scrum ceremonies like Daily Stand-ups and Sprint Reviews help teams communicate openly, resolve issues, and adapt quickly.

Focus on Results

High-performing teams focus on outcomes, not just tasks. They aim to create value for the customer and meet business goals. Success is measured by delivering a potentially shippable product increment that aligns with the customer's needs.

Accountability and Ownership

In Agile teams, accountability is collective. Every team member is responsible for meeting their commitments. Self-organizing teams hold each other accountable during Scrum ceremonies and remain focused on the Sprint goals.

Commitment to Continuous Improvement

High-performing teams continuously reflect and improve. They use retrospectives to discuss what worked, what didn't, and how to evolve. This culture of continuous improvement ensures teams adapt to new challenges and keep getting better.

Fun loving

Fun and happiness are essential for high-performing teams and boosting productivity. Shared laughter, celebrations, and enjoyable work environments strengthen bonds, reduce stress, and spark creativity, leading to greater engagement, resilience, and overall team success.

Metaphor: Think of a high-performing Agile team as a jazz band. The musicians are given the freedom to improvise and play their part, but each person is accountable to the others to create a harmonious and successful performance.

5.2 The Five Dysfunctions of a Team: Overcoming Common Obstacles

Patrick Lencioni's *The Five Dysfunctions of a Team* identifies common pitfalls that prevent teams from performing at their best. Here's how Agile teams can navigate these obstacles:

1. Absence of Trust

Without trust, teams cannot collaborate effectively. Trust is built through transparency and vulnerability. Agile teams establish trust during retrospectives and Sprint Planning, ensuring that members feel safe to express opinions, admit mistakes, and seek help.

2. Fear of Conflict

Healthy conflict is necessary for growth and innovation. High-performing Agile teams embrace constructive disagreements, using them to challenge ideas and improve solutions. Scrum ceremonies encourage open discussions, turning conflict into opportunities for better decisions.

3. Lack of Commitment

Commitment is essential for team alignment. In Agile teams, commitment is built during Sprint Planning when team members agree on the goals and tasks for the Sprint. This clarity ensures that everyone is on the same page and dedicated to achieving the goals.

4. Avoidance of Accountability

Accountability keeps the team on track. In Agile teams, accountability is encouraged through Daily Scrum, where members report on progress and blockers. Scrum Master and peers hold team members accountable for their commitments.

5. Inattention to Results

High-performing teams prioritize collective success over

individual agendas. They focus on delivering value to the customer. In Scrum, this is achieved by aligning Sprint goals with the business objectives and customer needs.

5.3 Conflict Resolution and Building a Collaborative Culture

Conflict is natural in any team, but it can be a powerful tool for growth if managed well. High-performing Agile teams know how to resolve conflicts constructively:

Encouraging Open Dialogue

Conflicts often arise from miscommunication or misunderstandings. High-performing teams encourage open, respectful conversations where issues are discussed honestly. Scrum ceremonies like Sprint Reviews and Retrospectives create space for these discussions.

Constructive Feedback

Effective conflict resolution in Agile teams involves feedback. Team members should feel comfortable giving and receiving constructive criticism. By focusing on the issue and not the individual, conflicts become opportunities for growth.

Mediation

Sometimes, conflicts may need mediation from the Scrum Master or another neutral party. The Scrum Master can facilitate conversations, helping team members reach mutual understanding and keep the team's focus on the goals.

Building Empathy

Building empathy within the team can prevent conflicts from escalating. High Emotional Quotient helps team members understand each other's perspectives, leading to better communication and stronger relationships. Teams that understand and respect each other's viewpoints can resolve conflicts quickly and effectively.

The *CARE* framework introduced in Chapter 2 can also be effectively applied to resolve conflicts.

Metaphor: Conflict resolution in Agile is like a sculptor chiselling away at a block of marble. What initially seems like a rough, unrefined object can, with time and care, become a masterpiece. By addressing conflicts head-on, teams can uncover better ways of working together and achieving their goals.

Building a high-performing Agile team requires more than just following Scrum practices. It is nurtured. It demands trust, open communication, accountability, and a shared commitment to continuous improvement. By addressing common dysfunctions, resolving conflicts constructively, and fostering a culture of growth, Agile teams can achieve exceptional performance. High EI, collaboration, and a focus on results create the foundation for sustained success. When teams work together with alignment and mutual respect, they can tackle complex challenges and deliver outstanding value.

Reflective Questions:

1. How does your team foster trust, and what can be done to improve it?
2. How does your team handle conflicts, and what steps can be taken to resolve them more constructively?
3. In what ways can your team improve its commitment to the Sprint goals and overall objectives?
4. How does your team ensure continuous improvement, and how can this process be enhanced?
5. What role does emotional intelligence play in improving communication and collaboration within your team?

Chapter 6
Agile Tools and Techniques for Teams

Agile frameworks thrive on continuous collaboration and adaptability, but the success of any Agile team relies on effective tools and techniques. These tools help teams stay organized, monitor progress, and ensure they deliver high-value outputs. In this chapter, we will focus on three key areas: Backlogs, User Stories, and Prioritization; Visualization Tools; and Agile Metrics. Each of these tools and techniques plays a vital role in guiding teams toward delivering customer-centric value in an iterative and transparent manner.

6.1 Backlogs, User Stories, and Prioritization

The backlog is a central tool in Agile that holds all the work that needs to be completed. It is the engine that drives the team's workflow. Within the backlog, user stories represent specific needs or features from the user's perspective. The process of backlog refinement, where teams regularly review and update the backlog, is essential for ensuring that the team is always working on the highest-priority tasks.

In Agile, the backbone of any project lies in managing the backlog. Think of a backlog as a to-do list, but instead of mundane household chores, it's a list of features, tasks, or user stories that define the product you want to build. The

Product Backlog contains all the features, enhancements, fixes, and tasks that need to be addressed, while the **Sprint Backlog** is a subset of items selected from the Product Backlog to be completed in a Sprint.

Backlog Refinement

Backlog refinement (or grooming) is a key practice where the team, along with the Product Owner (PO), reviews and revises the backlog to ensure that it remains relevant, prioritized, and well-defined. This is like cleaning up the list of items to focus on what truly matters, removing clutter, and ensuring that the team is always working on the highest-priority tasks. This activity can be planned during the Sprint as required.

User Stories

User stories are a tool for capturing functional requirements in a format that is easy for teams to understand and implement. A typical user story follows this simple format:

As a [user], I want [feature], so that [benefit].

For example: *As a customer, I want to track my order status online so that I can plan accordingly.*
User stories break down complex features into smaller, manageable tasks and serve as a reminder of the ultimate goal—the user's needs.

Prioritization

Prioritization ensures that teams focus on delivering the

most valuable work first. The Product Owner typically manages this process, selecting and arranging tasks in the backlog to maximize customer value. Various methods are used for prioritizing backlog items:

- **MoSCoW Method**: Categorizes requirements into four groups: Must-have, Should-have, Could-have, and Won't-have.
- **Value vs. Complexity**: High-value, low-complexity requirements are prioritized first, while low-value, high-complexity requirements are deferred.
- **Cost of Delay**: This concept helps Product Owner evaluate the financial impact of delaying certain requirements or tasks. It can be assessed using the **Weighted Shortest Job First (WSJF)** method, which calculates the cost of delay divided by the job duration, helping Product Owner prioritize requirements with the highest cost of delay per unit of effort for maximum customer satisfaction.
- **Kano Model**: The Kano model provides another framework for prioritizing requirements (features) by categorizing them into basic, performance, and excitement factors. Basic features are those that customers expect as standard, performance features are those that enhance customer satisfaction, and excitement features are those that delight customers and exceed expectations.

Metaphor: Prioritization is like planning a trip; you make sure to pack the essentials (must-haves), then the items that will enhance your experience (should-haves), followed by things that are nice to have (could-haves), and finally, you leave behind the unnecessary items (won't-haves).

6.2 Visualization Tools: Kanban Boards, Burn-Down Charts

Visualization tools provide clarity and transparency, helping Agile teams keep track of their work and progress. These tools not only make it easy to understand the current state of the project but also promote communication among team members and stakeholders.

Kanban Boards

Kanban boards are one of the most popular visualization tools used in Agile. A typical Kanban board is divided into columns such as "To Do," "In Progress," and "Done." Tasks or work items are represented as cards that move through these columns as the work progresses. The Kanban board aids in visualizing work, limiting work in progress (WIP), and ensuring that tasks are not started until others are completed—aligning with the key Kanban principle: "Stop starting, start finishing."

Metaphor: A Kanban board is like a conveyor belt in a factory. Items are processed step by step, ensuring smooth flow without overwhelming any part of the process.

Burn-Down Charts

A burn-down chart tracks the amount of work left to do over

the duration of a Sprint. It shows the progress toward the Sprint Goal, typically displayed as a graph that slopes downward as work is completed. This tool is vital for monitoring progress and ensuring that the team is on track to complete the work within the timebox. The Burn-Down chart should not be investigated in isolation.

Burn-Down charts come in various forms, such as Hours Burn-Down, Story Points Burn-Down, and Release Burn-Down. Some teams also utilize Burn-Up charts.

Metaphor: The burn-down chart is like a race against time. It shows how much time is left to finish the race, helping the team adjust their speed and approach if needed.

6.3 Agile Metrics:

Agile metrics are essential tools for measuring the performance of a team. These metrics help teams gauge their effectiveness, forecast future work, and identify areas for improvement. They are not just numbers; they provide valuable insights into how teams are functioning. However, it is important to remember that **working software is the primary measure of progress**, as stated in the Agile Manifesto. This principle highlights that the most significant indicator of success is delivering software that works and meets the customer's needs.

Velocity and Related Metrics

Velocity measures how much work a team can complete during a Sprint, usually expressed in Story Points (a unit of measure representing the effort required to complete a task). It's an important metric for forecasting future Sprint capacities. In addition to velocity, there are other related metrics that can provide deeper insights into team performance:

- **Throughput**: The number of user stories or tasks completed within a given time frame. It helps teams understand their capacity and plan future Sprints more effectively. This is better than the Velocity chart as it relies on actual work with reference to user stories or tasks.
- **Cycle Time**: The amount of time it takes for a task to move from "in progress" to "done." Shorter cycle times indicate a more efficient process.
- **Defect Density**: Measures the number of defects per unit of work. It helps teams assess the quality of their work and identify areas where improvements are needed.
- **Customer Satisfaction**: Ensure that your product meets customer expectations by gathering feedback and incorporating it into future iterations.

While velocity and related metrics are helpful for tracking progress, it's important to remember that no metric should be treated in isolation. A holistic view of the team's performance helps ensure a balance between speed and quality.

6.4 Definition of Ready (DoR) and Definition of Done (DoD)

While the Definition of Done (DoD) is a widely recognized concept in Agile, the **Definition of Ready (DoR)** is an equally important concept. Both are used to ensure that work is appropriately prepared before it begins and that it meets quality standards when it's finished.

Definition of Ready (DoR)

The Definition of Ready outlines the criteria that need to be met before a work item is moved into the Sprint. This includes ensuring that user stories are well-defined, have clear acceptance criteria, and are prioritized. Without a well-established DoR, work items can be ambiguous or incomplete, leading to delays and confusion.

Metaphor: Think of the DoR as a checklist before taking off on a flight. You ensure that everything is in place and ready for a smooth journey before you hit the "go" button.

Definition of Done (DoD)

The Definition of Done sets the criteria for when a task, user story, or bigger requirements is considered complete. It includes steps such as code being tested, reviewed, and integrated, documentation being updated, and product owners accepting the requirements. Having a clear DoD helps maintain quality, ensures consistency, and prevents work from being considered done when it is, in fact, incomplete. The stricter the Definition of Done (DoD), the better the quality, guiding the team toward high performance.

Metaphor: The DoD is like the final inspection at the end of an assembly line. Everything must pass quality checks before the product is ready for release.

Reflective Questions:
1. How do prioritization methods such as WSJF, MoSCoW, and Kano affect the team's ability to deliver value?
2. What are the benefits of using both Kanban boards and burn-down charts in tandem to monitor progress?
3. How do velocity, throughput, cycle time, and defect density help teams improve their processes and forecast future work?
4. What are the key benefits of having a clear Definition of Ready and Definition of Done?
5. How does your team currently use Agile metrics to measure performance, and how could this be improved?

Chapter 7
Delivering Value and Delighting Customers

In Agile frameworks, the ultimate goal is to deliver value to customers and stakeholders. However, it's not just about meeting expectations; it's about going beyond and creating memorable experiences that delight customers. This chapter delves into the strategies and techniques that teams can use to understand customer needs, deliver value, and move from basic satisfaction to customer delight.

7.1 Understanding Customer Needs and Value Delivery

Agile places a heavy emphasis on customer collaboration over contract negotiation, making it essential for teams to understand the real needs of their customers. Understanding customer needs is not a one-time task; it's an ongoing process that involves continuous engagement and learning.

Customer Needs Discovery

Customer needs go beyond what is explicitly stated. Often, customers are unable to articulate the underlying reasons for their requests. To truly understand their needs, Agile teams must leverage various techniques such as:

- **Empathy Mapping**: This tool helps teams understand

the thoughts, feelings, and Behaviours of their customers. By putting themselves in the customers' shoes, teams can uncover deeper insights.

- **Customer Interviews and Surveys**: Direct conversations with customers help clarify needs and expectations. Surveys can provide valuable quantitative data to identify patterns.
- **User Personas**: Developing detailed personas based on customer data helps the team focus on solving specific user problems, ensuring the product is designed for the right audience.
- **Journey Mapping**: This technique visually represents the customer's experience, helping teams identify pain points and opportunities to improve the product or service.

Delivering Value Through Incremental Progress

In Agile, value is delivered incrementally and iteratively, with each Sprint or iteration focusing on producing usable, working software. By breaking down the work into smaller, manageable chunks, teams can release features regularly, getting feedback early and often. This reduces the risk of delivering a product that doesn't meet customer expectations.

The key to delivering value is prioritizing work based on customer needs, business impact, and technical feasibility. This is where techniques like **MoSCoW, WSJF** and **Kano** can play a crucial role in making sure the team focuses on delivering the highest-value features.

Metaphor: Delivering value is like building a house one brick at a time. With each brick, you get closer to the final structure, and you can ensure the foundation is strong and well-aligned with customer expectations before moving to the next phase.

7.2 Incorporating Customer Feedback into the Agile Process

One of the core principles of Agile is responding to change over following a rigid plan. Feedback loops are essential to this flexibility, ensuring that the product evolves in line with customer needs and market dynamics.

The Feedback Loop

Customer feedback can be integrated into the Agile process at every stage, from planning to development, to testing and delivery. Regular, iterative feedback ensures that the team is always aligned with customer needs, and adjustments can be made as required.

- **Sprint Reviews**: During the Sprint Review, stakeholders and customers are invited to give feedback on the product increment. This feedback is valuable for making informed decisions about the next iteration.
- **Usability Testing**: Testing with real users provides actionable insights into how well the product meets user needs and where improvements can be made.
- **Surveys and Net Promoter Score (NPS)**: These tools

gauge customer satisfaction and gather insights into areas where the product can improve.

- **Customer Support Data**: Customer queries and complaints can provide direct insights into pain points that need to be addressed in future Sprints.

Closing the Feedback Loop

It's not enough to collect feedback; teams must act on it. Agile emphasizes continuous improvement, so when feedback is received, the team should analyse it, prioritize it, and incorporate necessary changes into upcoming iterations. By doing so, the team shows customers that their opinions are valued, which leads to better relationships and stronger customer loyalty.

Metaphor: Incorporating customer feedback is like adjusting a recipe. You keep tasting, adjusting the Flavours, and refining the dish until it satisfies the taste buds perfectly.

7.3 Moving from Customer Satisfaction to Customer Delight

Customer satisfaction is the baseline—it's about meeting expectations. But Agile teams should aim higher. True success lies in achieving **customer delight**, which involves exceeding expectations to create positive emotions and foster long-term loyalty.

Going Beyond Expectations

To move from satisfaction to delight, Agile teams must focus on delivering unexpected value. This goes beyond simply fulfilling requirements and instead involves surprising and delighting customers in meaningful ways.

1. **Anticipating Needs**: By analysing customer feedback and usage patterns, Agile teams can predict future needs before customers even express them. This proactive approach allows teams to offer solutions to problems customers didn't know they had, demonstrating foresight and care.

2. **Speed and Quality**: Delivering high-quality products faster than expected can leave a strong impression. Agile's iterative nature allows teams to roll out features quickly while maintaining quality, meeting the need for speed without compromising customer trust.

3. **Proactive Problem-Solving**: Address potential pain points before they surface. By continuously identifying areas for improvement, teams can create a seamless and worry-free experience that customers appreciate.

4. **Personalized Experiences**: Tailor your product or service to individual customer needs. For instance, providing preconfigured settings or customization options ensures customers feel their unique requirements are acknowledged and valued.

5. **Empowering the Customer**: Provide resources or tools that help customers succeed. For example, offering an analytics dashboard with actionable insights can empower them to make better decisions and maximize the product's value.

By embracing these practices, Agile teams can shift their mindset from merely satisfying customers to consistently delighting them. This not only strengthens customer loyalty but also fosters advocacy, turning delighted customers into passionate brand ambassadors.

Building Strong Relationships

Delighting customers isn't just about the product itself; it's about the experience surrounding it. Strong relationships are built on trust and consistent positive interactions. By continuously delivering value and responding to customer needs, teams can create a lasting bond with their customers.

Metaphor: Moving from satisfaction to delight in Agile is like tailoring a suit for someone—not just ensuring it fits (meeting expectations), but understanding their style, adding thoughtful details, and crafting it in a way that makes them feel truly seen and valued. It's the empathy in understanding their unspoken desires that transforms a good experience into an exceptional one.

Agile Principles and Customer Focus

Several **Agile Principles** emphasize customer value and responsiveness, reinforcing the approach to delivering value and delighting customers. Several principles directly support these goals:

- **Early and continuous delivery of valuable software:** By delivering usable increments frequently, customers receive value early and can provide feedback to keep the product aligned with their needs.

- **Welcome changing requirements:** This principle highlights the importance of embracing change based on evolving customer needs or market conditions, ensuring the product stays relevant and valuable.
- **Deliver working software frequently:** Frequent delivery allows for early validation, reduces risk, and ensures that teams are always aligned with the customer's expectations.
- **Close collaboration:** Close collaboration ensures that the development process stays focused on customer priorities and fosters shared understanding between teams and stakeholders.
- **Simplicity – Deliver what matters most:** By focusing only on what adds value, teams avoid unnecessary features, delivering leaner, more effective products that meet customer expectations.

Agile Values in Customer Delight

Agile values further underscore the importance of **responding to change** and putting customers at the centre of the process:

- **Individuals and Interactions over Processes and Tools**: Prioritizing people—both team members and customers—ensures that communication and collaboration foster deeper understanding and trust.
- **Customer Collaboration over Contract Negotiation**:

By engaging customers continuously throughout the project, Agile teams ensure that the end product aligns with customer needs and exceeds expectations.

- **Responding to Change over Following a Plan**: Agile values adaptability and responsiveness to change, enabling teams to incorporate new customer insights and adjust products as required.

Reflective Questions:

1. How do you ensure that customer needs are effectively understood and addressed throughout the Agile process?
2. In what ways can you improve your team's customer feedback loop to ensure that changes are made in response to actual user input?
3. What actions can your team take to move from merely satisfying customers to truly delighting them?
4. How can the Agile principles of collaboration and transparency be leveraged to improve customer relationships and trust?
5. How does your team respond to change in customer requirements, and how do you ensure that the customer is at the centre of this process?

Chapter 8
Navigating Complexity in a VUCA World

In the fast-moving currents of today's business environment, organizations face constant waves of volatility, uncertainty, complexity, and ambiguity—what we refer to as a VUCA world. Just as a skilled captain navigates a ship through unpredictable seas, Agile provides the tools to steer teams and organizations through these turbulent waters. In this chapter, we will explore how Agile can serve as a compass for managing uncertainty, a rudder for complexity, and a lifeboat for resilience.

8.1 Volatility and Uncertainty: Agile as a Solution

Imagine you're sailing across an ocean, and the weather is unpredictable, with sudden storms and shifting winds. A traditional, rigid approach to navigation might fail, leaving the ship vulnerable to the next squall. Agile, on the other hand, is like a seasoned captain who knows how to adjust the sails, steer the rudder, and keep the crew focused, no matter what the weather brings.

Key Concepts:
- **Agile Mindset**: Agile is the adaptable sail that catches whatever wind comes its way. It ensures that the ship stays on course despite the unpredictable gusts of volatility. It is built on the foundation that change is

constant, and the ability to adjust direction quickly is paramount.

- **Responding to Change**: Just as a sailor tacks the ship to adjust to the wind's shifting directions, Agile allows teams to continuously adjust to the market's changing demands. By viewing change as an opportunity, teams sail toward growth rather than struggle against it.
- **Feedback Loops**: The feedback from the crew on deck serves as real-time information for the captain, guiding decisions to adjust the sails and course. In Agile, these feedback loops—such as daily stand-ups or sprint reviews—ensure that the team remains aligned and responsive to new challenges.

Strategies for Implementation:
- Equip your team with the Agile mindset, encouraging flexibility and adaptability in every decision. The Love for Unknown should be part of team culture.
- Foster short, continuous feedback cycles to help adjust the course early and often.
- Empower the team to make decisions quickly based on the latest available data, just as a captain would adjust the ship's course according to changing wind conditions.

8.2 Managing Complexity Through Iterative Learning

Navigating through complexity is akin to crossing a foggy,

uncharted sea. You can't see the entire coastline from the ship's deck, but you can use smaller navigational points—lighthouse beams, stars, and landmarks—to guide your way. Agile helps you manage this complexity by breaking down the journey into smaller, iterative learning loops, making the fog clearer with each step.

Key Concepts:
- **Iterative Development**: Agile allows teams to take small, manageable steps forward, rather than attempting to cross the entire ocean in one leap. Like a ship mapping its course one checkpoint at a time, iterative development helps teams focus on achieving manageable goals and gaining insights along the way.
- **Incremental Progress**: Each sprint is like a short leg of a journey, with each step providing more clarity about the broader destination. Just as every inch of progress on a ship brings you closer to shore, every increment of development brings your team closer to its goal.
- **Empowered Teams**: In Agile, teams are not passive passengers—they are active navigators of their own journey. By breaking complex tasks into bite-sized chunks, teams are better able to assess progress, adjust their sails, and learn from their course.

Strategies for Implementation:
- Break down complex projects into smaller, iterative

cycles, similar to smaller, manageable sailing routes.
- Create space for frequent learning and course correction after each iteration.
- Empower teams to continuously review their progress and make real-time decisions that align with the team's broader goals.

8.3 Building Resilience in Teams and Organizations

Resilience in a VUCA world is like the anchor that keeps a ship steady in a storm. While the waves of volatility and uncertainty may rock the boat, a strong anchor allows the ship to regain balance. Similarly, Agile builds organizational resilience by promoting continuous learning, adaptability, and emotional fortitude.

Key Concepts:
- **Agile Resilience**: Resilience is not about avoiding the storm; it's about riding the waves. Agile practices, such as regular retrospectives, ensure that teams are continuously improving, learning from setbacks, and strengthening their collective resolve, like a well-built ship that can weather any storm.
- **Collaboration and Support**: In an Agile environment, teams work together like a well-coordinated crew. When the sea gets rough, it's the crew's ability to communicate, collaborate, and support one another that keeps the ship afloat.
- **Psychological Safety**: Building resilience is also about

creating a safe space where individuals can take risks without fear of blame. It's like a ship's crew who knows that even if a mistake happens during the journey, it will be an opportunity to learn and improve for the next leg of the voyage.

Strategies for Implementation:
- Foster a culture of continuous learning and improvement by holding regular retrospectives, where teams review what went well and what didn't.
- Promote cross-functional collaboration, ensuring that team members can lean on each other's strengths during times of stress.
- Create a psychologically safe environment where failure is seen as an opportunity for growth and innovation, just as sailors learn from each journey's challenges.

Reflective Questions:
1. How do you handle sudden changes or unpredictable situations in your current role? Are you more like a rigid sailor who resists the wind, or a flexible one who adjusts the sails?
2. Can you identify a complex challenge you are currently facing? How can you break this down into smaller, iterative steps to move forward without feeling overwhelmed?
3. What practices can you introduce to ensure you and

your team learn from failure and remain steady despite external pressures?

4. How does the iterative nature of Agile help teams navigate volatility and uncertainty?

5. Reflect on a time when you faced a major challenge in a project. How could Agile's iterative learning process have helped you address that challenge more effectively?

6. What strategies can you implement to ensure your team remains adaptable and responsive in a VUCA world?

Chapter 9
Ensuring Quality and Adaptation

Quality and adaptability are essential to Agile processes. In today's fast-paced environment, where customer expectations and market conditions change rapidly, delivering high-quality products while remaining flexible is key. This chapter explores how to integrate quality into Agile, the importance of continuous delivery and improvement, and how the principle of "Inspect and Adapt" leads to sustained success.

9.1 Integrating Quality into Agile Processes

In Agile, **quality is not an afterthought**—it is embedded at every stage of the process. Instead of catching defects at the end, Agile teams prioritize **preventing issues** before they occur. Quality becomes a shared responsibility of the entire team, driving consistent value and trust.

Here are key practices to ensure quality:

- **Clear Acceptance Criteria**: Before development starts, well-defined acceptance criteria clarify what "success" looks like. This aligns the team on quality expectations and ensures features meet customer needs.

- **Test-Driven Development (TDD)**: Developers write tests before coding, ensuring functionality works as expected from the start. TDD promotes clean, reliable code and reduces bugs.
- **Behaviour-Driven Development (BDD)**: Through collaboration between developers, testers, and stakeholders, BDD defines the application's Behaviour in user-friendly terms. This ensures the product aligns with user needs and business goals.
- **Continuous Integration (CI)**: Frequent integration of code changes, combined with automated testing, identifies defects early. CI ensures that the software remains in a **working, deployable state** at all times.
- **Definition of Done (DoD)**: The DoD acts as the team's quality checklist. It ensures work is "done" only when it meets agreed standards, including passing tests, code reviews, and documentation updates. This avoids surprises at the end of a Sprint.
- **Automated Testing**: Automation is the backbone of Agile quality. Tests—unit, integration, and regression—are automated to deliver quick, reliable feedback. Teams can release with confidence, knowing the product is stable and functional.
- **Code Reviews**: Peer reviews foster learning, catch defects early, and ensure adherence to coding standards. This collaborative practice boosts quality and shared ownership.
- **Continuous Feedback Loops**: Agile teams leverage

frequent feedback—through reviews, retrospectives, and customer validation—to refine their processes and outputs continuously.

- **Pair Programming**: Two developers work together on the same code, with one writing the code and the other reviewing it in real-time. This approach reduces defects, promotes knowledge sharing, and ensures higher code quality.

- **Mob Programming:** The entire team collaborates on a single task at the same time, using one computer. This technique enhances shared understanding, improves problem-solving, and boosts the overall quality of the solution.

- **Exploratory Testing**: Testers go beyond pre-defined test cases to explore the application, identifying edge cases and unexpected behaviours. This practice uncovers hidden defects and improves system robustness.

- **Static Code Analysis:** Automated tools analyse the codebase for potential issues, such as security vulnerabilities, coding standard violations, or performance bottlenecks. This ensures adherence to best practices.

- **Incremental Refactoring**: Teams regularly refactor the code to improve its structure, readability, and maintainability without altering its functionality. This prevents technical debt and keeps the codebase healthy over time.

- **Shift-Left Testing:** Quality checks, including testing, are integrated early in the development process. This practice reduces defects later in the cycle and lowers the cost of fixing issues.

- **Feature Toggles**: Teams use feature toggles to deploy code to production even if certain features are incomplete. This enables safe experimentation, faster delivery, and smoother rollbacks.
- **Cross-Functional Pairing:** Developers pair with testers or business analysts to ensure shared understanding of requirements, quality goals, and test cases, improving the overall product quality.

Metaphor: Quality in Agile is like tending a garden. You don't wait until the end of the season to pull weeds. Instead, you water, prune, and inspect regularly, ensuring steady growth and a thriving result.

In Agile, quality is a team responsibility. Everyone— **developers, testers, and the Product Owner**—works together to ensure that the product is of the highest quality. The **Scrum Master** fosters an environment where quality flourishes and a strong, collaborative culture takes root. This **collaborative approach** creates an environment where issues are identified and resolved quickly.

9.2 Continuous Delivery

Continuous Delivery (CD) ensures that the product is always in a **deployable state**—tested, validated, and ready for release at any time. Instead of waiting for big, risky deployments, Agile teams release small increments frequently, keeping customers engaged and delivering value faster.

In CD, every feature or fix undergoes automated testing and integration before it's considered complete. This not only reduces errors but also creates a smooth, predictable release process.

Benefits of Continuous Delivery:

- **Faster Feedback**: Frequent releases allow for immediate validation, ensuring teams build what customers truly need.
- **Lower Risk**: Small, incremental deployments minimize the chances of failure and make it easier to fix issues quickly.
- **Steady Value Flow**: Customers benefit from new features and improvements sooner, creating consistent value delivery.

Metaphor: Continuous Delivery is like running a **well-oiled assembly line**. Each part (feature) is inspected and refined at every station, ensuring the final product meets the highest standards without delays or rework.

By embracing CD, Agile teams don't just deliver software—they **accelerate outcomes**, adapt to change swiftly, and build trust through reliability. It's a game-changer for delivering **quality at speed**.

9.3 Leveraging "Inspect and Adapt" for Sustained Success

"Inspect and Adapt" is one of the most powerful principles in Agile. It encourages teams to regularly review their work, reflect on their methods, and adjust their processes based on feedback and new insights.

Why "Inspect and Adapt" matters:
- **Frequent reflection:** Regular Scrum events like **Daily Scrum**, **Sprint Reviews** and **Retrospectives** offer teams the opportunity to inspect their progress, adapt their strategies, and continuously improve.
- **Data-driven decisions:** Teams use data from metrics like velocity, defects, and customer feedback to make informed decisions about how to improve.
- **Customer involvement:** Feedback from customers and stakeholders during the Sprint Review helps guide the team in the right direction.

Metaphor: Imagine a gardener regularly checking the plants in a garden. By inspecting the plants and adapting their care (watering, trimming, etc.), the gardener ensures the plants grow strong and healthy. Similarly, "Inspect and Adapt" allows teams to continuously improve their product and process.

Collaboration and Communication for Quality.
Quality is not just about technical practices. **One team, close**

collaboration, and face-to-face communication are also vital components in achieving high-quality outcomes. In Agile, teams work closely together, sharing knowledge and resolving issues in real time.

- **Cross-functional teams:** Agile teams are typically cross-functional, meaning team has all the skills necessary to deliver the product. Developers, testers, and other specialists collaborate seamlessly throughout the Sprint, leveraging their collective expertise to enhance the quality of the product.
- **Face-to-face communication:** Agile emphasizes the importance of direct communication over written documentation. In co-located teams, face-to-face conversations help solve problems faster and create a shared understanding of the project.
- **Collaboration with stakeholders:** The **Product Owner** and the team actively engage with the stakeholders, ensuring that the product meets customer needs. This close collaboration allows the team to prioritize work effectively and adapt to changes quickly.

Metaphor: Think of a successful sports team. The players (team members) communicate constantly, adapt to the game (product), and adjust their strategy together. The coach (Scrum Master) ensures the team stays focused on the ultimate goal—winning (delivering value).

By embedding quality into every aspect of the Agile

process—through strong engineering practices like TDD and BDD, continuous delivery, and close collaboration—Agile teams can ensure that they deliver products that not only meet customer needs but are also adaptable to future changes. The ongoing practice of **"Inspect and Adapt"** helps ensure that teams continue to improve and deliver value, year after year.

Reflective Questions:
1. How can practices like **TDD** and **BDD** improve the quality of your team's output?
2. What impact would **continuous delivery** have on the speed and quality of your team's work?
3. How can **face-to-face communication** improve the quality of collaboration and decision-making in your team?
4. How does **Inspect and Adapt** help your team improve both its product and processes over time?
5. In your experience, how does the **Definition of Done** contribute to maintaining quality standards?

Chapter 10
Implementing Agile in an Organization

Implementing Agile in an organization is like setting the sails of a ship to catch the wind, helping you navigate toward your goals more effectively. Agile is not a goal in itself, but rather a tool—like the compass—that helps you achieve your ultimate destination: delivering value, improving collaboration, and responding quickly to change. Agile encourages flexibility, transparency, and continuous improvement, but its successful implementation requires thoughtful planning, commitment, and cultural alignment within your organization. The organization must determine which Agile framework is best suited to achieving its goals. In this chapter, we'll explore how to implement Scrum within your organization to set the right course and ensure successful navigation.

10.1 Implementation steps

1. Assess Organizational Readiness

Before setting sail with Scrum, it's crucial to assess whether your organization is ready for this journey. Think of it like checking the condition of your ship, the weather, and the crew before leaving the harbour. Without the right preparation, you may find yourself facing choppy waters.

Key Areas to Assess:

- **Leadership Support**: Like a captain steering the ship,

leadership plays a crucial role in guiding and supporting the Scrum transformation. They must understand Scrum's value and provide the necessary resources and encouragement.

- **Cultural Readiness**: Scrum thrives in environments where collaboration, transparency, and adaptability are valued. Is your organization's culture open to change and continuous improvement, or does it prefer to stick to traditional ways?
- **Current Processes**: Scrum requires a flexible approach, so it's important to understand your existing workflows. Are your processes too rigid and bureaucratic? Can they accommodate Scrum's iterative and adaptive nature?

2. Define Clear Objectives and Expectations

Defining clear objectives is like charting your course before heading out to sea. Without a clear destination, your ship may end up adrift, aimlessly floating without purpose. Clearly articulate why you are adopting Agile and what you aim to achieve with it.

Common Objectives Include:

- **Faster Time to Market**: Deliver products and services more quickly by working in short, iterative cycles. Think of Scrum as a journey broken down into manageable steps, helping you reach milestones faster.
- **Increased Collaboration**: Scrum fosters a collaborative environment across teams and

departments. Just like a well-coordinated crew working together toward a common goal, Scrum enhances communication and teamwork.

- **Enhanced Product Quality:** Ensure higher quality outputs by embedding quality practices such as continuous testing, peer reviews, and clear acceptance criteria throughout the development process.
- **Improved Adaptability:** Enable teams to respond effectively to changing requirements and market conditions, ensuring the organization remains competitive and relevant.
- **Greater Transparency:** Foster an environment where progress, challenges, and updates are openly shared, creating trust among teams and stakeholders.
- **Maximized Value Delivery**: Focus on delivering the most valuable features first by prioritizing tasks that have the highest impact on customers and business outcomes.
- **Continuous Improvement**: Establish a culture of learning and improvement through retrospectives, feedback loops, and iterative refinements to processes and products.
- **Increased Employee Engagement**: Empower teams through self-organization and decision-making, leading to higher job satisfaction, motivation, and retention.
- **Cost Efficiency**: Reduce waste and optimize resource usage by focusing only on necessary work, ensuring

the budget is used effectively.

- **Scalable Practices**: Build processes and practices that can be scaled across multiple teams and projects, enabling organizational growth without losing agility.
- **Predictability and Risk Management**: Improve the predictability of deliverables and manage risks more effectively through incremental deliveries and regular feedback cycles.
- **Alignment with Strategic Goals**: Ensure that team efforts align with the organization's long-term vision and strategic objectives by maintaining a clear connection between work and business priorities.
- **Better Customer Satisfaction**: By regularly incorporating customer feedback and delivering working product increments, Scrum helps create products that better meet customer needs, much like navigating toward a destination guided by customer preferences.

3. Begin with Training and Education

Like setting up the right equipment for your journey, proper training and education are essential to make Scrum work in your organization. Knowledge of Scrum principles and roles ensures that the team knows how to operate the ship smoothly and efficiently.

Key Areas of Training:

- **Scrum Fundamentals**: Ensure that everyone understands Scrum's principles, roles, and ceremonies. Like familiarizing the crew with their duties, everyone must understand their role in the Scrum process.

- **Role-Specific Training**: Scrum Masters, Product Owners, and Development Teams all have unique responsibilities. Role-specific training ensures everyone understands what's expected of them and how they contribute to the Scrum framework.
- **Leadership Training**: Develop leadership skills at all levels to empower teams foster trust, and drive alignment. Workshops can cover servant leadership, decision-making, emotional intelligence, and conflict resolution.
- **Team Collaboration and Communication**: Train teams on effective communication techniques, conflict management, and collaboration strategies to ensure smooth interactions and stronger teamwork.
- **Agile Mindset and Culture**: Educate teams and leaders on adopting an Agile mindset, emphasizing adaptability, customer focus, and continuous improvement to align behaviour with Agile values and principles.
- **Tools and Techniques**: Equip teams with the right tools to manage workflows and track progress. Tools like Jira, Trello, or Monday.com are like the navigational instruments that help you stay on course.

4. Start Small and Scale Gradually
The sea can be unpredictable, and diving into the deep end

with Scrum can be overwhelming. Instead, it's wise to start small, testing Scrum with a few teams before expanding it organization-wide. This gives you time to adjust the sails and refine the process without committing to a massive overhaul all at once.

Steps to Start Small:

- **Test and Learn**: Start with one or two teams to experiment with Scrum. Use this pilot phase to learn what works well and what needs adjustment.
- **Gather Feedback**: Collect feedback from these initial teams to understand what challenges they face and how processes can be improved. This feedback helps refine the Scrum implementation.
- **Show Results**: Early wins and successes in pilot teams help build momentum and demonstrate the value of Scrum to other teams and leadership.

5. Foster a Culture of Collaboration and Transparency

Scrum operates on trust, openness, and constant communication. Imagine a ship crew where each member shares progress, obstacles, and ideas. Without open communication, the ship might veer off course, and teamwork can break down. Creating a culture of collaboration and transparency is essential for Scrum to succeed.

Encouraging Collaboration:

- **Collaborative Problem-Solving Workshops:** Hold workshops where team members collectively address challenges or brainstorm solutions. These sessions bring diverse perspectives together and create a shared sense of ownership.

- **Cross-Functional Collaboration:** Actively involve developers, testers, product owners, and other stakeholders in discussions. Cross-functional interactions ensure that expertise from different areas is leveraged to create well-rounded solutions.
- **Shared Accountability:** Promote a culture where success and failure are shared by the team, not individuals. This approach strengthens trust and encourages team members to support each other.
- **Transparency Through Visual Tools:** Use Kanban boards, information radiators, and burndown charts to ensure everyone has a clear view of progress, priorities, and potential bottlenecks. Visible progress fosters open dialogue and better planning.
- **Team Agreements:** Establish agreements on communication norms, decision-making processes, and conflict resolution. When everyone understands and aligns on collaboration guidelines, the team functions more effectively.

6. Empower Cross-Functional Teams

In Scrum, the teams are like self-sufficient crew members, each with the necessary skills to navigate the project from start to finish. Empowering cross-functional teams means they no longer need to rely on others outside the team, allowing them to work more efficiently and make faster decisions.

Empowering Teams:
- **Diverse Skillsets**: Ensure teams are equipped with the necessary knowledge across all areas (design, development, testing, etc.), enabling them to deliver the full product increment by themselves.
- **Autonomous Decision-Making**: Teams should be able to make decisions without waiting for approval from leadership. Giving them autonomy fosters ownership and responsibility for delivering results.
- **End-to-End Ownership**: Empower teams to take full responsibility for the product increment, from inception through development and delivery. Just like a ship crew taking full responsibility for the vessel's journey, teams own the product's progress.

7. Measure and Monitor Progress

Just as a ship needs navigational tools to track progress, Scrum requires continuous measurement to stay on course. Regularly monitor progress with key metrics to ensure you're heading in the right direction and make adjustments as needed.

Refer to section 10.1.2 to establish metrics that align with your objectives. Additionally, consult Chapter 6 to determine the appropriate metrics to monitor progress and success.

10.2 Common Challenges to Agile

Adopting Agile is transformative, but organizations face common hurdles during implementation. Addressing these challenges is key to success.

1. Resistance to Change
The Challenge:
Employees and leaders accustomed to traditional ways of working often resist change. Agile demands a mindset shift, moving from fixed processes to adaptability, collaboration, and iterative delivery.
How to Overcome:
- Clearly communicate *why* Agile is being adopted and the benefits it brings.
- Involve key stakeholders early and provide training and coaching.
- Leadership should model Agile Behaviours to inspire the team.

2. Lack of Understanding of Agile Principles
The Challenge:
Organizations may focus too much on frameworks (Scrum, Kanban) without truly embracing Agile values like collaboration, adaptability, and delivering customer value.
How to Overcome:
- Start with training on Agile *mindsets* and *principles* before tools.
- Foster a culture that values feedback, collaboration, and learning.
- Encourage leadership to embody Agile principles.

3. Poorly Defined Roles

The Challenge:

Agile roles such as Scrum Master, Product Owner, and Team Members are often misunderstood, leading to confusion, misaligned responsibilities, and inefficiency.

How to Overcome:

- Clearly define roles, responsibilities, and accountability.
- Provide role-specific training.
- Promote collaboration among Scrum Master, Product Owner, and team members.

4. Misaligned Expectations and Goals

The Challenge:

Senior leadership often expects quick, predictable results, which may conflict with Agile's iterative and flexible approach.

How to Overcome:

- Set realistic expectations about Agile's incremental delivery model.
- Promote transparency through sprint reviews and demonstrations.
- Align goals and timelines with Agile values of delivering continuous value.

5. Inadequate Communication and Collaboration

The Challenge:

In organizations with silos or distributed teams, lack of communication impedes Agile success, causing misalignment and delays.

How to Overcome:
- Break down silos with daily standups, retrospectives, and collaborative planning sessions.
- Implement tools (like Slack, Jira, or Zoom) to facilitate communication.
- Foster an open, transparent culture where feedback flows freely.

10.3 Common Pitfalls to Avoid

When adopting Agile, it's easy to fall into traps that undermine success. Avoiding these common pitfalls can ensure smoother Agile transformation.

1. Treating Agile as a Silver Bullet
The Pitfall:
Believing Agile will instantly solve all problems without addressing deeper organizational issues.
How to Avoid:
- Understand Agile is a mindset shift, not a quick fix.
- Commit to continuous improvement, patience, and adaptation.

2. Lack of Executive Buy-In
The Pitfall:
Without leadership support, teams lack resources, training, and direction to succeed with Agile.
How to Avoid:
- Educate leaders on Agile principles and their role in supporting the transformation.

- Make leaders champions of Agile change.

3. Over-Focus on Tools and Frameworks
The Pitfall:
Prioritizing tools (like Jira) and frameworks over the core Agile values of collaboration, adaptability, and customer focus.
How to Avoid:
- Use tools as enablers, not drivers of Agile.
- Regularly revisit Agile principles to ensure alignment.
- Tailor the tools to fit your needs, rather than adjusting your needs to fit the tools.

4. Skipping Cultural Change
The Pitfall:
Implementing Agile practices without addressing the organization's culture often leads to resistance and failure.
How to Avoid:
- Promote a culture of trust, empowerment, and continuous learning.
- Encourage decentralized decision-making and team autonomy.

5. Not Embracing Incremental Delivery
The Pitfall:
Organizations continue to focus on big-bang deliveries rather than iterative, incremental progress.
How to Avoid:
- Break large goals into smaller deliverables.

- Focus on delivering a Minimum Viable Product (MVP) and iterating based on feedback.

10.4 Strategies to Address Stakeholder Concerns

Stakeholder concerns are common during Agile adoption, as it demands a significant shift in mindset and practices. Proactively addressing these concerns ensures smoother implementation and stakeholder buy-in. Below are **five proven strategies** to address stakeholder concerns effectively:

1. Communicate the Benefits of Agile

Stakeholder Concern: *"How will Agile benefit my project or the organization?"*

Strategy:
Educate stakeholders on how Agile delivers tangible benefits tailored to their priorities. Demonstrate how Agile improves collaboration, reduces risks, accelerates delivery, and enhances product quality through continuous feedback.

- **Tailored Communication:** Customize messages for stakeholders at different levels.
    - *Leaders*: Highlight cost savings, faster time-to-market, and ROI.
    - *Teams*: Focus on reduced pressure, improved workflows, and team collaboration.
- **Use Real-World Examples:** Share success stories or case studies where Agile has delivered measurable

results in similar contexts or industries.

2. Involve Stakeholders Early and Often

Stakeholder Concern: *"I won't have enough control or visibility over the project's progress."*

Strategy:
Engage stakeholders early and throughout the Agile process to ensure visibility, control, and alignment with business goals. Agile emphasizes collaboration, enabling stakeholders to actively participate and shape outcomes.

- **Sprint Reviews and Demos:** Invite stakeholders to observe progress, provide feedback, and see tangible results after each iteration.
- **Regular Feedback Loops:** Integrate stakeholder suggestions consistently to demonstrate responsiveness and build trust.
- **Transparency:** Use tools like visual dashboards or burndown charts to showcase project status, upcoming tasks, and risks in real time.

3. Manage Expectations with Transparent Communication

Stakeholder Concern: *"I'm worried about scope creep and lack of control over deliverables."*

Strategy:
Set clear expectations about Agile's iterative delivery model

and emphasize how it focuses on delivering high-priority outcomes.

- **Define Clear Goals:** Collaborate with stakeholders to set measurable goals aligned with organizational priorities.
- **Explain Iterative Delivery:** Emphasize Agile's approach to delivering working software incrementally, which helps monitor progress and adjust priorities.
- **Scope Management:** Highlight the role of the Product Backlog in prioritizing and managing evolving requirements without losing control.

4. Address Concerns About Change Resistance

Stakeholder Concern: *"Agile seems like a big change. I'm worried about disrupting the existing workflows."*

Strategy:
Mitigate change resistance by demonstrating Agile's adaptability, offering support, and creating a gradual transition plan.

- **Pilot Agile:** Start with a small team or project to demonstrate success before scaling across the organization.
- **Training and Support:** Educate stakeholders on Agile concepts, roles, and processes to build confidence.
- **Identify Change Champions:** Empower advocates who can influence others by showcasing the benefits

of Agile within their teams.

5. Demonstrate Agile's Structure and Flexibility

Stakeholder Concern: *"Agile seems chaotic and lacks structure. How can we ensure we meet deadlines and achieve results?"*

Strategy:
Clarify that Agile combines discipline with flexibility, ensuring predictable delivery while adapting to changing priorities.

- **Explain Frameworks:** Share how Agile operates within structured frameworks (e.g., Scrum, Kanban) with defined roles, ceremonies, and processes.
- **Set Iterative Timelines:** Highlight Agile's short cycles (sprints) with clear deliverables, making progress predictable and measurable.
- **Mitigate Risks:** Emphasize practices like continuous testing, reviews, and retrospectives that identify and address issues early, ensuring deadlines are met.

Reflective Questions

1. How ready is your organization to embrace Scrum, and what changes are needed to create a supportive environment?
2. Are the leadership and teams aligned on the value and goals of adopting Scrum?
3. How well does your team embrace the Agile mindset

beyond tools and processes, and where do you see gaps between principles and practice?

4. What recurring challenges (e.g., resistance, communication gaps, role confusion) are slowing your Agile journey, and how can you systematically address them?

5. How actively are stakeholders and leadership engaged in supporting and enabling your Agile practices, and what can you do to gain more alignment?

6. What challenges might you face in the Scrum adoption process, and how can you address resistance effectively?

7. What specific training and support will help your teams succeed in adopting Scrum?

Chapter 11
Agile in Practice – Case Studies

Agile is not just a theoretical concept—it's a practice that has transformed organizations across various industries. In this chapter, we will explore real-world examples of how Agile has been applied in small teams, large enterprises, and non-tech industries, demonstrating its power to drive efficiency, foster collaboration, and deliver results.

11.1 How Small Teams Succeed Using Scrum

Small teams, like small boats on a vast ocean, face unique challenges and opportunities. They may not have the scale of larger teams, but their agility and flexibility can often allow them to deliver faster, with more personalized solutions. Let's explore a real-world example of a small team using Scrum to overcome these challenges.

Case Study: Spotify's Small Teams (Squads)
Spotify, the music streaming giant, is known for its unique use of Agile in managing teams. The company's product development is broken down into small, autonomous teams called "squads." Each squad operates like a mini-startup within the larger company, responsible for specific features or services. Each squad uses Scrum to manage their work—following sprints, daily standups, and retrospectives.
Outcome:

- Spotify's ability to scale its product offerings without losing flexibility has been a key driver of its success.
- Teams can innovate rapidly, with the freedom to choose the best technology and process that fits their goals.
- This small-team model has helped Spotify reduce bureaucracy and increase cross-functional collaboration.

Key Takeaways:
- Small teams, when empowered and given autonomy, can be more agile and efficient.
- Scrum provides the structure to ensure accountability and deliverables while maintaining the flexibility to innovate.
- The Spotify model demonstrates that Agile practices like Scrum can thrive in small, cross-functional teams.

11.2 Agile Transformation in Large Enterprises

Large enterprises are like massive ships navigating through the vast ocean of the market. Changing their course requires coordination, leadership, and clear direction. Agile transformation in such organizations requires a fundamental shift in culture, mindset, and processes, which can be challenging but ultimately rewarding. Here's a look at how one large enterprise implemented Agile successfully.

Case Study: ING Bank's Agile Transformation
ING, one of the largest banks in the world, faced significant challenges in adapting to the rapidly changing financial

services landscape. The company needed to become more responsive to customer needs, faster at delivering new features, and better at collaborating across departments. ING's Agile transformation started by restructuring into cross-functional teams called "tribes," "squads," and "chapters," modelled after the Spotify model.

By embracing Agile principles across the organization, ING broke down silos between departments, redefined roles (e.g., Product Owners, Scrum Masters), and used Scrum and Kanban to improve the flow of work. The transformation was supported by extensive leadership buy-in, and teams were trained on Agile methodologies.

Scaling is not the Focus of This Chapter:
Although large enterprises like ING have successfully embraced Agile, scaling Agile across such large organizations presents additional complexities. This book does not delve deeply into scaling frameworks, but it is important to note that there are several established frameworks designed specifically for scaling Agile, such as:

- **SAFe (Scaled Agile Framework)**: A comprehensive framework for scaling Agile across multiple teams, focusing on alignment, collaboration, and delivery of value.
- **LeSS (Large Scale Scrum)**: A simple, lightweight framework that extends Scrum principles to multiple teams, focusing on improving collaboration and reducing overhead.
- **Scrum@Scale**: A flexible scaling framework built on

the core Scrum principles, designed to scale Scrum across multiple teams.

- **DAD (Disciplined Agile Delivery)**: A process decision framework that supports the adoption of Agile practices at scale, focusing on the most appropriate Agile methods for specific needs.

Key Takeaways:
- Scaling Agile requires additional frameworks and methodologies tailored to large organizations, but the core principles of Agile remain the same.
- SAFe, LeSS, Scrum@Scale, and DAD are among the most popular frameworks for scaling Agile practices, each with its unique features.
- While scaling is crucial for large enterprises, the true benefit of Agile comes when **all departments**—from HR to marketing to finance—embrace Agile principles. Agile is not just an IT or software development process; it must be a holistic, organization-wide shift for it to truly succeed.

Outcome:
- ING reduced its time-to-market for new products by 30%.
- Teams became more self-sufficient, improving their ability to respond to customer needs without waiting for approval from higher-ups.
- ING reported improved employee satisfaction and collaboration across departments.

Key Takeaways:
- Agile transformation in large enterprises requires clear leadership, a shift in mindset, and proper training across all levels of the organization.
- The use of cross-functional teams (tribes, squads) can help break down silos and improve collaboration.
- Agile allows large organizations to be more flexible, innovative, and customer-focused, but to unlock its full potential, it must span across all departments and functions, not just IT.

11.3 Agile Applied in Non-Tech Industries

Agile is not just for tech companies—its principles have been applied with great success in a variety of industries. Non-tech industries, like healthcare, marketing, and even manufacturing, are discovering the value of Agile's iterative, customer-focused approach. Here's a real-world example of how Agile was successfully implemented in a non-tech setting.

Case Study: The UK's National Health Service (NHS) – Agile in Healthcare

The NHS in the UK faced long patient wait times, inefficiencies in service delivery, and a lack of collaboration between departments. To tackle these issues, the NHS implemented Agile practices in various parts of the organization, focusing on improving patient care and administrative processes. One notable example was the introduction of Scrum to manage patient intake and administrative work in hospital emergency departments. By adopting Scrum, teams could focus on small, manageable tasks during each sprint, continuously improving the intake process. The Product Owner in this context was typically a lead nurse or doctor, while the Scrum Master was a healthcare operations specialist. This structure helped improve communication and ensure that everyone involved in the process was aligned on goals.

Outcome:
- Patient wait times in emergency departments were reduced by 20%.
- Healthcare teams worked more collaboratively, which improved morale and the quality of care.
- The iterative approach allowed the teams to respond quickly to bottlenecks or patient complaints, improving the overall experience.

Key Takeaways:
- Agile's iterative approach is valuable even in non-tech environments like healthcare, where continuous improvement is critical.
- Cross-functional collaboration between clinicians and administrative staff ensures a holistic approach to solving problems.
- Agile can improve efficiency, reduce waste, and enhance customer satisfaction in non-tech industries

as well.

By looking at real-world examples from Spotify, ING Bank, and the NHS, we can see that Agile is a flexible and powerful approach that transcends industries. Reflecting on these case studies and asking the questions above will help you consider how you can apply Agile practices in your own environment to drive tangible results.

Reflective Questions:
1. How can you implement Scrum in your own small team to increase productivity and communication? What are the key benefits of working in short sprints for your team's goals?
2. In your organization, how can you create a strong case for Agile transformation? What leadership steps are necessary to ensure this shift is successful at a large scale?
3. Can Agile principles improve processes in your industry (even if it's not tech-based)? How can you implement iterative cycles and cross-functional collaboration in your organization to enhance outcomes?
4. What are the key differences between scaling Agile in small teams versus large enterprises? If your organization is large, how can you start introducing scaling frameworks while ensuring that all departments adopt Agile practices?

Chapter 12
Agile Beyond Work: Making It a Way of Life

Agile isn't just a framework for work; it can be a mindset that enriches your entire life. Imagine living with the same principles that drive successful teams and projects in the workplace—flexibility, collaboration, and continuous improvement—and applying them to your personal growth, relationships, and health. Just as Scrum helps teams adapt and thrive in the face of change, so can it help you navigate the various aspects of your life. In this chapter, we explore how Agile principles can transform your approach to life, making you more adaptable, intentional, and resilient.

12.1 Applying Agile Principles in Personal Growth

Agile principles, grounded in flexibility, feedback, and continuous improvement, can transform personal development. Think of your growth like a Sprint—small, focused efforts that help you move toward your goals while adjusting as you go. Instead of rigid plans, embrace the iterative process, refining your approach based on what you learn.

Steps to Apply Agile in Personal Growth:
- **Embrace Iteration**: Personal growth is a journey that doesn't have a final destination. Break your goals into small, manageable tasks or "Sprints." After each Sprint, reflect on what worked and what didn't, adjusting as needed.
- **Set Clear Priorities**: Similar to creating a product backlog, identify the most important aspects of your life that need attention. Whether it's learning a new skill, improving relationships, or enhancing physical health, focus on what matters most.
- **Continuous Feedback**: Seek feedback from others and from your own reflections. Just like regular retrospectives in Scrum, use feedback to make improvements and refine your personal growth journey.
- **Adaptability**: Life is full of unexpected changes, and being Agile means staying flexible and adapting when necessary. Your goals and strategies might need to evolve based on new experiences or external challenges.

By viewing your personal growth through the lens of Agile, you stop seeing setbacks as failures and start seeing them as opportunities to iterate, learn, and improve.

12.2 Agile for Family, Learning, and Health Goals

Agile isn't just for teams at work—it can be applied to various personal areas such as family, learning, and health goals. Think of each aspect of your life as its own project, with its own goals, timelines, and evolving requirements.

Agile for Family:

- **Communication and Collaboration**: Just as Scrum relies on regular communication between teams, Agile principles in family life encourage regular check-ins, shared responsibilities, and collaboration. Hold weekly family standups to align on tasks and expectations and have retrospectives to discuss what went well and where improvements can be made.

- **Iterate on Family Activities**: When planning family activities or routines, be open to adapting them as you go. If a certain activity isn't working, don't be afraid to pivot and try something different. This approach can help keep family life dynamic and enjoyable.

- **Reflect and Learn:** After any family event, take time to reflect on two simple yet powerful questions. These questions encourage meaningful conversations and help identify what worked, what could be improved, and why. By capturing these insights, you create a foundation for smoother, more enjoyable future events.

  1. What went well?
  2. If we had a chance to do it again, what would we change?

Agile for Learning:

- **Incremental Learning**: Break your learning goals into

small, bite-sized tasks. Just as Scrum emphasizes delivering small increments of value, set achievable milestones in your learning journey. This helps you avoid feeling overwhelmed and allows you to celebrate small wins along the way.

- **Sprint Reviews for Learning**: After completing a module or topic, conduct a review of what you've learned. What worked well in your study habits? What can be improved for the next learning sprint?

Agile for Health:

- **Track Small Wins**: Health goals are much easier to achieve when broken into small, achievable actions. Start with small daily tasks—like drinking more water or exercising for 10 minutes—and build from there. Regularly assess your progress and adjust as needed.
- **Health Retrospectives**: After a week of following your health routine, reflect on what went well and what could be improved. This process can help you stay on track and make necessary changes for better health outcomes.

By applying Agile to family life, learning, and health, you create a continuous improvement mindset that makes everyday challenges more manageable and fulfilling.

12.3 The Journey of Lifelong Agility

Agility is not just a destination; it's a lifelong journey. Just as Scrum is an ongoing process of continuous improvement, so too is personal and professional growth. Lifelong agility means being open to change, learning from each experience, and constantly striving to improve in every aspect of life. It's about building resilience in the face of challenges and being flexible enough to adapt to whatever comes your way.

The Agility Journey:
- **Continuous Improvement**: Lifelong agility is rooted in the idea of never being "done" with improvement. Every situation, whether personal or professional, presents an opportunity to refine your approach and develop further.
- **Embrace Change**: Change is inevitable, but with agility, you can embrace it as an opportunity for growth. Whether it's a new job, a new family dynamic, or a shift in health goals, agility means staying adaptable and learning to thrive amid uncertainty.
- **Learning from Experience**: Like any Scrum team that holds regular retrospectives, take time to reflect on your experiences. What worked well in your life? What didn't? What changes can you make to improve going forward?

Lifelong agility isn't about always being perfect—it's about constantly striving to improve, iterate, and adapt to the changes that life throws at you.

12.4 Real-Life Stories of Agile Leadership

Agile leadership is about staying flexible, responsive to change, and continuously improving. Here are some real-world leaders who embody these principles in their work:

Story 1: Indra Nooyi – Iterative Transformation at PepsiCo
As CEO of PepsiCo, Indra Nooyi adopted an iterative approach to transform the company's portfolio toward healthier products. She introduced the "Performance with Purpose" strategy, focusing on sustainability and health-conscious offerings. This transformation wasn't a single, massive shift but a series of phased changes, including reformulating products to reduce sugar and launching new health-focused brands. Nooyi continually sought feedback from consumers and stakeholders, refining the strategy over time. Her leadership reflects the essence of Agile — responding to change and evolving based on data and feedback.

Story 2: Elon Musk – Innovation Through Rapid Iteration
Elon Musk is known for embracing rapid iteration at **SpaceX** and **Tesla**. At SpaceX, Musk's team famously followed the "fail fast, learn fast" philosophy. Rather than perfecting designs first, they built prototypes and launched them quickly, learning from each failure. This approach led to numerous successful missions after early setbacks. Similarly, Tesla's **over-the-air software updates** are continuously pushed to vehicles, improving performance and features

over time.

Story 3: Jeff Bezos – Customer-Centric Agility

Jeff Bezos's leadership at Amazon is a prime example of **customer-centric agility**. Bezos famously said, "We're willing to be misunderstood for long periods of time." Amazon started as an online bookstore but, with constant feedback loops, it evolved into an e-commerce titan, and later a cloud computing powerhouse with **AWS**. The company's commitment to continuous experimentation has helped it pivot and expand quickly in response to changing customer needs.

Story 4: Satya Nadella – Growth Mindset at Microsoft

When Satya Nadella took over as CEO of Microsoft, he transformed the company's culture by introducing a **growth mindset**. Nadella encouraged Microsoft to be more agile by embracing failure and **continuous learning**. A key example was Microsoft's shift to **cloud computing**, where he led the company's transformation toward services like **Azure**, despite initial internal resistance. Nadella's approach prioritized iteration and adapting to changing technologies.

Story 5: Richard Branson – Agility in Entrepreneurship

Richard Branson's approach to leadership is rooted in embracing new opportunities with agility. For example, in his **Virgin Galactic** venture, Branson adapted to technical setbacks by learning from them, continuously improving the designs for commercial space travel. Branson's willingness to pivot when necessary—such as moving from record stores to airlines, then to health care—shows his adaptability, and his ability to innovate quickly in response to market needs.

Reflective Questions:
1. How can you apply Agile principles of iterative learning and feedback to your personal leadership style?
2. What aspects of your life or work can benefit from more experimentation and a "fail fast, learn fast" approach?
3. How do you ensure that you are staying adaptable and responsive to changing circumstances, much like leaders like Elon Musk and Jeff Bezos?
4. What personal projects or initiatives can you start applying Agile principles to improve outcomes and progress?
5. How do you foster a culture of continuous improvement and learning within you own team or organization, like Satya Nadella at Microsoft?

Chapter 13
Future of Agile & Next Steps

As organizations worldwide continue to embrace Agile practices, the future of Agile holds exciting opportunities for individuals and businesses alike. Agile is no longer confined to software development—it is rapidly expanding into new domains such as education, healthcare, finance, and even personal life. In this chapter, we explore emerging trends, valuable certifications, and steps you can take to prepare for your own Agile journey.

13.1 Future Trends in Agile

The Agile movement is evolving in response to changing business landscapes and technological advancements. Here are key trends shaping the future of Agile:

- **Enterprise-Wide Agility**: Agile is moving beyond individual teams to drive business agility at all organizational levels. Frameworks like SAFe, LeSS, and Disciplined Agile are helping large enterprises implement Agile practices across departments.
- **Agile in New Domains**: Industries like education, healthcare, and manufacturing are leveraging Agile to improve efficiency and customer satisfaction. Schools are experimenting with Agile principles to enhance learning outcomes, while hospitals use Agile to streamline patient care processes.

- **AI and Agile**: Artificial Intelligence (AI) is revolutionizing Agile processes. From automating repetitive tasks to analysing team performance, AI tools enhance decision-making, reduce cycle times, and improve outcomes.
- **Hybrid Models**: Many organizations are adopting a mix of Agile and traditional project management (Waterfall) to suit their unique needs. Hybrid models allow teams to combine flexibility with predictability.
- **Focus on Value Delivery**: Agile will continue to emphasize delivering value over just completing tasks. Organizations are shifting from project-centric to product-centric mindsets, focusing on continuous customer satisfaction and outcomes.

13.2 Certifications and Learning Paths

Certifications provide a structured way to validate your Agile knowledge and skills. Here are key certifications to help you advance in your Agile journey:

1. **Certified ScrumMaster (CSM)**
   - Ideal for beginners to understand the fundamentals of Scrum.
   - Offered by Scrum Alliance, this certification covers roles, events, and artifacts of Scrum.
2. **PMI Agile Certified Practitioner (PMI-ACP)**
   - Recognized globally, this certification focuses on a wide range of Agile methodologies, including Scrum, Kanban, Lean, and XP.

    o It is perfect for those looking to demonstrate versatility in Agile practices.

3. **SAFe Agilist (Leading SAFe)**
   - For professionals working in large enterprises implementing the **Scaled Agile Framework (SAFe)**.
   - This certification helps individuals lead Agile transformations at scale.

4. **Professional Scrum Master (PSM)**
   - Offered by Scrum.org, the PSM is an advanced alternative to CSM. It emphasizes a deeper understanding of Scrum principles and applications.

5. **ICAgile Certifications**
   - ICAgile offers role-specific certifications such as Agile Coaching, Agile Team Facilitation, and Business Agility, allowing individuals to specialize further.

6. **Kanban Management Professional (KMP)**
   - Focuses on Kanban principles for visualizing workflows, limiting work-in-progress, and improving delivery efficiency.

Choosing the Right Certification:
- If you're just starting out, **CSM** or **PSM I** is a great entry point.
- For those managing scaled Agile in large enterprises, **SAFe Agilist** is highly valuable.
- To broaden your understanding of multiple Agile

methodologies, **PMI-ACP** is a robust choice.

Building an Agile skillset requires continuous learning. Beyond certifications, engage with Agile communities, attend conferences, and participate in workshops to stay current with trends.

13.3 Preparing for Your Agile Journey

Adopting Agile is more than learning frameworks—it's about embracing a mindset that prioritizes flexibility, collaboration, and value delivery. Here's how you can prepare for your Agile journey:

- **Assess Your Starting Point**: Identify where you stand in terms of Agile knowledge and experience. Are you a beginner or an experienced professional looking to deepen your expertise?
- **Learn the Fundamentals**: Start with foundational concepts such as the Agile Manifesto, Scrum roles, events, and artifacts. Understanding these basics ensures a strong Agile foundation.
- **Choose Your Path**: Whether you aspire to become a Scrum Master, Agile Coach, or Product Owner, select a path that aligns with your goals. Certifications can help validate your expertise.
- **Start Small and Iterate**: Apply Agile principles to small projects, whether at work or in personal endeavours. Experiment, learn, and improve incrementally.

- **Seek Feedback**: Like regular retrospectives in Scrum, reflect on your progress and seek feedback from peers or mentors. Adjust your approach as needed.
- **Build Connections**: Join Agile meetups, communities, or forums to interact with professionals, share experiences, and gain new perspectives. Platforms like LinkedIn, Meetup, and Scrum Alliance are great places to start.
- **Focus on Mindset, Not Just Process**: Agile is about embracing change, fostering collaboration, and prioritizing people over processes. Developing an Agile mindset is the key to lasting success.

13.4 Final Thoughts: Building an Agile Future

Agile is not a passing trend—it's a proven approach to achieving success in an ever-changing world. As organizations embrace agility, the role of Agile professionals becomes even more critical. Whether you're helping a team adopt Scrum, scaling Agile across an enterprise, or applying Agile principles to your personal life, you are shaping the future.

To build an Agile future:

- **Be Adaptable**: Embrace change and use it as an opportunity to learn and grow.
- **Focus on Continuous Improvement**: Agile is a journey, not a destination. Commit to learning, iterating, and improving every day.
- **Prioritize Value**: Always aim to deliver outcomes that

truly matter—whether for customers, teams, or yourself.

The future belongs to those who can adapt quickly, collaborate effectively, and deliver value continuously. By committing to lifelong agility, you position yourself as a leader ready to navigate whatever the future holds.

As you embark on your Agile journey, remember it's not about perfection, but about continuous growth. Embrace the challenges, learn from failures, and keep refining your approach. The world of Agile is full of potential, and the future is yours to shape.

Let's build an Agile future together—one step at a time.

Reflective Questions:
1. What Agile certification or learning path aligns best with your career goals?
2. How can you start applying Agile principles to your current work or personal projects?
3. What steps can you take to embrace a continuous improvement mindset?
4. How can you build stronger connections with Agile professionals and communities?
5. What does building an Agile future mean to you, and how can you contribute to it?

❈ ❈

Thank you for taking the time to explore this book.

I hope this book provided you with valuable insights and practical tools to enhance your journey in Agile project management.

To stay updated with the latest trends, tips, and insights in Agile and project management, I invite you to connect with me on LinkedIn. By joining my network, you'll also receive updates about new courses, resources designed to deepen your Agile expertise, workshops, and live Q&A sessions

Let's build a community of Agile enthusiasts who are passionate about growth and continuous learning.

Scan this QR code, or
use link: https://www.linkedin.com/in/rahulshahcoach/

Looking forward to engaging with you and sharing ideas that shape the future of Agile!

Warm regards,
Rahul Shah
Certified Agile Trainer and Author

133

Appendix A: Glossary of Terms

Here's a glossary of key Agile terminologies that are used in this book:

Acceptance Criteria

A set of predefined conditions that a product or deliverable must satisfy to be accepted by stakeholders.

Agile Manifesto

A declaration of values and principles for Agile software development, emphasizing collaboration, customer satisfaction, and responsiveness to change.

Backlog

A prioritized list of tasks, features, or requirements for a product, maintained and updated regularly by the team or product owner.

Burndown Chart

A visual representation of the amount of work remaining versus time, used to track project progress in Agile.

Daily Scrum (Daily Stand-Up)

A short daily meeting where team members discuss progress, impediments, and plans for the day.

Definition of Done (DoD)

A checklist of criteria that must be met for a product or

feature to be considered complete.

Definition of Ready (DoR)

A checklist of criteria that must be met before a work item is started, ensuring clarity and preparedness.

Feature

A large user story that can be broken down into smaller, more manageable stories for implementation.

Increment

A usable piece of the product delivered at the end of a sprint, representing progress toward the final deliverable.

Kanban

An Agile methodology that visualizes work items on a board to optimize workflow and manage tasks efficiently.

Product Owner (PO)

A key role in Agile responsible for maximizing the value of the product and managing the product backlog.

Scrum

A popular Agile framework that emphasizes iterative development, time-boxed sprints, and team collaboration.

Sprint

A fixed period, usually 1–4 weeks, during which the team completes a specific set of tasks or user stories.

Sprint Planning

A meeting held at the beginning of a sprint to plan the work and identify goals for the sprint.

Sprint Retrospective

A meeting at the end of a sprint where the team reflects on what went well, what didn't, and how to improve.

Sprint Review

A session where the team demonstrates the work completed during the sprint to stakeholders for feedback.

Story Points

A relative unit of measure used to estimate the effort required to complete a user story.

User Story

A short, simple description of a feature or requirement written from the perspective of an end user.

Velocity

The amount of work a team can complete in a sprint, measured in story points or tasks.

WIP (Work in Progress)

The number of tasks or work items being worked on at any given time, often limited in Kanban to ensure smooth workflow.

Appendix B: Resources

Books:
1. Schwaber, Ken, and Jeff Sutherland. *The Scrum Guide*. Scrum.org, 2020.
2. Cohn, Mike. *Succeeding with Agile: Software Development Using Scrum*. Addison-Wesley, 2010.
3. Beck, Kent. *Extreme Programming Explained: Embrace Change*. Addison-Wesley, 1999.
4. Lencioni, Patrick. *The Five Dysfunctions of a Team: A Leadership Fable*. Jossey-Bass, 2002.
5. Sutherland, Jeff. *Scrum: The Art of Doing Twice the Work in Half the Time*. Crown Business, 2014.

Articles and Websites:
1. Manifesto for Agile Software Development - https://agilemanifesto.org/
2. The History of Agile Software Development - https://www.cprime.com/resources/what-is-agile/
3. Agile vs Waterfall: Key Differences Explained - https://www.atlassian.com/agile/project-management/waterfall-vs-agile
4. Growth Mindset: How to Develop a Love for Learning - https://www.mindsetworks.com/
5. How Emotional Intelligence Can Improve Team

Dynamics - https://www.forbes.com/

6. Scrum Guide - https://www.scrumguides.org/

7. Scrum Events and Artifacts Explained - https://www.scrum.org/resources/scrum-guide

8. The Power of Iterative Development in Agile - https://www.mountaingoatsoftware.com/

9. Kaizen in Agile: Continuous Improvement for Teams - https://www.agilealliance.org/glossary/continuous-improvement/

10. Building High-Performing Agile Teams - https://www.atlassian.com/agile/teams

11. The Five Dysfunctions of a Team: Overcoming Team Obstacles - https://www.patricklencioni.com/the-five-dysfunctions/

12. Kanban Boards and Agile Metrics - https://www.atlassian.com/agile/kanban

13. The Importance of DoR and DoD in Scrum - https://www.scrumalliance.org/

14. Incorporating Customer Feedback into the Agile Process - https://www.productplan.com/glossary/customer-feedback/

15. How to Move Beyond Customer Satisfaction to Delight - https://hbr.org/

16. Using Agile to Navigate Complexity and Uncertainty - https://www.infoq.com/agile/

17. Resilience in Agile Teams - https://www.agilealliance.org/